The Deen Fallacy: How the West Came to Misclassify Islam

Cause, Consequence and Correction

Elaine Ellinger

The Deen Fallacy: How the West Came to Misclassify Islam
Cause, Consequence, and Correction

ISBN Paperback: 978-1-0698472-5-6
ISBN eBook: 978-1-0698472-6-3

Published by POI Books
www.poi-nps.com

This printing includes additional historical material on early modern toleration, France, and the export of Islamic personal law beyond India.

Previous Works by the Author:

The Hidden Curriculum of Islamic Schools: From Prayer to Sharia – a Child's Indoctrination. POI Books, 2026

Constitutional Integrity and Equal Citizenship in India / भारत में संवैधानिक अखंडता और समान नागरिकता POI Books, 2026

Un Bilan Civilisationnel: Comprendre la Menace, Reprendre l'Avenir (Vol. 1-3) POI Books, 2025-2026

A Civilizational Reckoning: Understanding the Threat, Reclaiming the Future. POI Books, 2025

Timeless Essays About Islam and Its Doctrine: What It Includes and Why It Matters. POI Books, 2024

Contents

DISCLAIMER

This book examines the historical classification of Islam in the West, the consequences of that classification, and the doctrinal foundations of the Islamic deen as presented in its own primary sources. It analyses the Quran, hadith, classical jurisprudence, and related materials in order to clarify concepts that have been widely misunderstood or mistranslated.
The purpose is public education and policy analysis. Readers are encouraged to verify all references independently. The critique is directed at doctrines, legal structures, institutional practices, and ideological systems – not at race or ethnicity.

All quotations are reproduced for criticism, review, research, and educational analysis.

Preface

For years I studied Islamic doctrine directly from its primary sources. Then I turned to the textbooks actually used to educate Muslim children in the West. What struck me was not merely the content, but the language – the consistent, careful way Muslim children are taught about deen, jihad, zakat, Mohammed's legal precedent, and the all-encompassing nature of Sharia. It bore little resemblance to the softened, fragmented picture of Islam most Western readers encounter through English translations, media, and policy documents.

That gap raised a more fundamental question: not "What is Islam?" but "How did the West come to misunderstand it so badly?" How did generations of scholars, translators, and institutions shape the way Islam is perceived, explained, and ultimately accommodated in the West?

The consequences of this linguistic and conceptual mismatch are now visible in daily life: parallel societies, growing social friction, eroded trust, and increasing pressure on free speech. When people lack the necessary vocabulary to accurately describe what is happening to their communities, frustration builds. The result is not merely intellectual confusion. It is social breakdown, followed by demands for more restrictions on discussion – the very mechanism societies need to correct course.

Precise terminology is therefore not pedantry. Words like deen (as opposed to "religion"), creedism, and recognizing the full scope of Sharia are essential tools. They allow citizens and policymakers to think clearly and speak honestly. Without them, democratic societies are left increasingly unable to defend themselves through reason, debate, and law – until less civilized options begin to look inevitable.

This book examines how that profound misunderstanding took root and became entrenched in Western scholarship and institutions. It also confronts the Islamic doctrine itself – the element so often missing or softened in public discussion – and traces where that doctrine is quietly steering successive generations. It is written for those who sense that something fundamental is shifting in our civilization, but who have not yet been given the words to name it.

A Note on Sources

Throughout this book, references are drawn from the same authorities used by Islamic scholars themselves: the Quran; the major hadith collections; the classical biographies of Mohammed (Sira); the early histories and commentaries of al-Tabari, Ibn Ishaq, and Ibn Kathir; and standard legal manuals such as Reliance of the Traveller, a Classic Manual of Islamic Sacred Law. These are not external or hostile sources. They are the texts that define the deen of Islam from within (see glossary).

Glossary of Familiar and Unfamiliar Terms and Phrases

While the Islamic Ummah shares a common doctrinal vocabulary understood throughout much of the Muslim world, many non-Muslims have long suffered not only from an inadequate understanding of exactly what Islam is, but also through the persistent use of terms both familiar and unfamiliar – that have one understanding to those who practice Islam, and an entirely different or benign meaning for those who don't. While the former population is aware of both meanings and their effect on the latter, the opposite is not true. This has allowed the gaslighting of large swaths of the populace for many centuries.

Words such as authority, freedom, good, human rights, innocent, justice, peace, religion, terror, and truth often carry meanings within Islamic doctrine that differ significantly from those commonly understood in the West. Other terms - such as deen, Sharia, Jihad, Ummah, and Kafir - are translated into English in ways that obscure rather than clarify their Islamic meaning and significance.

The result has been centuries of misunderstanding – a misunderstanding that Islamic law itself produced by restricting non-Muslim access to the texts from the outset. Quran 56:79 and 9:28, together with classical rulings that forbid non-Muslims from touching or teaching the Quran, established the barrier. Reliance of the Traveller (k1.2e) requires that anyone for whom a Quran is purchased must be Muslim; the same rule applies to books of hadith and any work containing even a slight amount of the Quran.

Today, however, widespread digital communication, unprecedented access to foundational Islamic texts in English, and higher levels of education provide an opportunity to examine these terms in the context of the doctrine from which they arise.

Note: In this book, "constitutional" refers to systems based on secular law, equal citizenship under a single legal framework, and the supremacy of man-made law over any religious or ideological code.

***

Abrogation (Naskh)
The Islamic doctrine and legal principle that allows later Medina revelations to supersede earlier Meccan verses, based on Quran 2:106. Used to resolve contradictions and determine legal rulings.

Adhan
The Islamic call to prayer, recited five times daily. Beyond announcing the prayer, the Adhan proclaims core Islamic beliefs, including that there is no god but Allah and that Mohammed is the Messenger of Allah. It serves as a public affirmation of the Islamic deen and its authority.

Allah
The one God of Islam. In Islamic doctrine, Allah is the ultimate source of authority. His commands, as revealed in the Quran and through the example and orders of Mohammed (the Messenger), take precedence over human legislation.

Alms or Charity
See Zakat. Zakat is one of the Five Pillars of Islam. Unlike voluntary charity, it is a compulsory Islamic tax with eight prescribed categories of recipients, including those engaged in jihad in the Cause of Allah (fi sabil Allah) (Quran 9:60).

Apostasy
Leaving or abandoning Islam. Under classical Islamic jurisprudence, apostasy by a sane adult Muslim is punishable by death.

Authority
Ultimate authority belongs to Allah. Mohammed is the supreme human authority in Islam, and his example (the Sunnah), together with the Quran, forms the basis of Sharia.

Believer
In Islamic doctrine, a person who has submitted to Allah and His Messenger, accepts the Quran as the literal word of Allah, and follows Sharia as revealed through Mohammed. The term carries legal and social implications, distinguishing believers from unbelievers (kafirs).

Brotherhood (Ikhwan)
Primarily membership in the Ummah. The Quran describes believers as brothers (Quran 49:10), reflecting a relationship based on shared deen rather than nationality or ethnicity.

Cause of Allah (fi sabil Allah)
Literally, "in the cause (or path) of Allah." A recurring Quranic expression referring to actions undertaken to advance Allah's deen. Depending on the context, it encompasses dawa, migration (hijrah), spending wealth, and jihad in its various forms, including by the mouth, the pen, wealth, and the sword. It is one of the eight categories eligible to receive zakat (Quran 9:60).

Classical (Islamic Jurisprudence)
In Islamic studies, classical refers to the foundational body of Islamic legal interpretation developed by the recognized schools of jurisprudence. The term does not mean obsolete, archaic, or no longer applicable.

Communal Obligation (Fard Kifayah)
An obligation imposed on the Muslim community as a whole rather than on every individual. If a sufficient number of Muslims fulfil the obligation, it is no longer obligatory on the others. If no one fulfils it, then "everyone who is aware that it is obligatory is guilty of sin." Such obligations include jihad, dawah, enjoining what is right and forbidding what is wrong, the administration of Sharia, and the establishment and maintenance of the caliphate (Reliance of the Traveller o25.2). These obligations ultimately serve the objective of making Allah's deen prevail over all others (Quran 9:33; 48:28; 61:9).

Community. See Ummah.

Creedism (alt. spelling Creedism)
Prejudice, discrimination, or unequal treatment resulting from classifications derived from creed rather than from neutral constitutional or universal principles.

Creedist
A person, institution, or policy that practises or facilitates Creedism.

Darura
A principle in Islamic law meaning necessity. It renders forbidden acts lawful when a Muslim is compelled by need, it also functions as a flexible legal tool that lets Muslims temporarily suspend obligations for social convenience, political strategy, or to protect Islam's interests. However, once an Islamic alternative becomes available – i.e. finance – then Muslims are expected to use it (Quran 2:173, 5:3, 6:119, 16:115).

Deception
The concealment or selective presentation of information to achieve a permitted objective. Classical Islamic jurisprudence sanctions deception in certain circumstances.

Deen
A comprehensive system of submission and obedience to Allah governing worship, law, politics, economics, commerce, family life, personal hygiene, morality, and society. The term appears approximately one hundred times in the Quran and consistently describes Islam as a deen rather than a religion in the modern Western sense. It encompasses both belief and the legal, political, and social order established by Allah. The Quran states that Allah sent Mohammed with "guidance and the deen of truth" to make it prevail over all other deen (Quran 9:33, 48:28, 61:9), underscoring its comprehensive and governing nature. (Arabic plural: adyān)

Dhimmi
A non-Muslim living under Islamic rule who pays the jizyah tax and accepts subjugation under Sharia. Lacks legal equality and full civil rights.

Disbeliever. See Kafir.

Dualism (Doctrine)
Islamic doctrine recognizes that all Quranic revelation remains true, yet different passages may be applied according to circumstances. Meccan verses revealed when Islam is politically weak and Medinan verses revealed after political and military ascendancy are both authoritative. In practice, the former are often emphasized when Muslims are a minority, while the latter govern where Islamic authority is established. This principle exists alongside abrogation (naskh), whereby later revelations may supersede earlier ones in matters of law.

Dualism (People)
Sharia classifies people into distinct legal categories, each with its own rights, obligations, protections, and penalties. The primary distinction is between believers and unbelievers, but

different rules also apply to men and women, free persons and slaves, Muslims living under Islamic rule and non-Muslim subjects (dhimmis), and other recognized classes. A person's legal position depends upon the category to which he or she belongs.

Equal Rights

Islamic educational materials frequently state that men and women have equal rights. In classical Islamic doctrine, however, equality refers to equal spiritual worth and accountability before Allah, while legal rights and obligations under Sharia differ in areas such as inheritance, testimony, marriage, divorce, personal autonomy, guardianship, and leadership.

Fatwa

An Islamic legal opinion issued by a qualified jurist (mufti) interpreting and applying Sharia. Millions are issued annually in response to questions submitted by ordinary Muslims from anywhere in the world on matters ranging from personal conduct and family life to finance, medicine, politics, and jihad (including warfare). A Muslim in Canada can readily obtain a fatwa from a jurist in Cairo or elsewhere. Muslims may follow the rulings of their own jurist or those of another whom they regard as authoritative. This system provides legal guidance throughout the global Ummah and illustrates that the Islamic deen governs far more than worship alone.

Fiqh

Islamic jurisprudence; the interpretation and application of Sharia based on the Quran, Hadith, legal reasoning (qiyas), and scholarly consensus (ijma) – all of which must align with the primary texts (Quran and Hadith) and cannot contradict them.

Fitrah

The innate human disposition to submit to Allah and follow

Islamic belief and behaviour (Quran 30:30). According to Islam, all people are born Muslim, which is why converts are sometimes called "reverts." Practices such as circumcision, are considered part of maintaining the fitrah (Muslim 2658d; Bukhari 5891)

Fitna

Disorder, temptation, or unrest. Used to refer both to sexual temptation (especially involving women) and to social or political disruption that threatens Islamic authority.

Free / Free woman

In the modern West, freedom generally refers to individual liberty protected by law. In Islam, freedom is understood as liberation from man-made authority through submission to the will and law of Allah. Quran 33:59 requires Muslim women to veil so they are recognised as free, not servants or whores (Ibn Kathir tafsir).

Good

Conduct that conforms to the commands of Allah and advances the objectives of the deen. Muslims are instructed to "race to all that is good." (Quran 2:148)

Governance

The ordering of society according to Allah's revealed law (Sharia), rather than legislation derived solely from human authority.

Guidance

Direction provided by Allah through the Quran and the example of Mohammed. Guidance consists in following the straight path (Sharia) revealed by Allah.

Hadith

Reports describing the words, actions, approvals, and

characteristics of Mohammed. Together with the Quran, the authentic hadith collections form the primary textual foundation of the Sunnah and Sharia. Sunni Islam recognizes six canonical collections - Sahih al-Bukhari, Sahih Muslim, Sunan Abi Dawud, Jami' al-Tirmidhi, Sunan al-Nasa'i, and Sunan Ibn Majah - while Shia Islam recognizes four principal collections. Only the six canonical Sunni collections are cited in this book.

Halal
Determines what is permissible under Sharia. Although commonly associated with food, the term applies to finance, commerce, contracts, marriage, slavery, personal conduct, and many other aspects of life. Opposite of Haram.

Haram
Forbidden under Sharia. Opposite of halal. Includes certain foods, behaviours, and associations.

Hijra
Mohammed's migration from Mecca to Medina in 622 CE. marking the beginning of the Islamic calendar. The term also refers to migration undertaken in the cause of Allah, including relocation to strengthen or advance the Muslim community.

- The Messenger of Allah said: "There is no migration (hijra) after the Conquest, but there is jihad and intention. And when you are called out to fight, then go forth." (Bukhari 2783).

House of Worship
A common Western description of a mosque. Historically, the mosque has also functioned as the religious, judicial, educational, political, military, communications, and administrative centre of the Islamic community.

Human Rights
Rights derived from Allah and defined by Sharia rather than by universal human equality. Classical Islamic jurisprudence assigns different rights and obligations according to legal status, including distinctions between Muslims and non-Muslims, men and women, and free persons and slaves.

Innocent
In Islamic doctrine, innocence is not understood solely as the absence of criminal wrongdoing. Disbelief (kufr) itself is considered a serious moral fault and an enormity. Unbelievers (kafirs) are described as corrupt (Quran 3:118; Reliance of the Traveller o24.3-4).

Islam
Literally, submission to Allah. In the Quran, Islam is presented as the final and complete deen, the system revealed to govern both individual conduct and society as a whole. (Quran 5:48)

Jahiliyyah
Literally "ignorance" or "the age of ignorance." In Islamic doctrine, the term refers not only to pre-Islamic Arabia but also to societies, laws, customs, or systems that do not conform to the rule of Allah as expressed through Islam and Sharia.

Jihad: (From Reliance of the Traveller, o9.0)
'Jihad means to war against non-Muslims, and is etymologically derived from the word mujahada, signifying warfare to establish the religion.

- "Fighting is prescribed for you" (Quran 2:216)
- "Slay them wherever you find them" (Quran 4:89)
- "Fight the idolators utterly" (Quran 9:36)
- Bukhari: "I have been commanded to fight people until they testify that there is no god but Allah and that Muhammad is the Messenger of Allah, and perform the

prayer, and pay zakat. If they say it, they have saved their blood and possessions from me, except for the rights of Islam over them. And their final reckoning is with Allah."

- Muslim: "To go forth in the morning or evening to fight in the path of Allah is better than the world and what is in it."'

Islamic sources also describe jihad as being carried out by various means, including the mouth, the pen, wealth, migration (hijra), and armed struggle.

Jurist
An Islamic scholar qualified to interpret and apply Sharia. Jurists issue legal rulings (fatwas) in response to questions submitted by Muslims on every aspect of life. Today, many provide this guidance internationally through websites, email, and other online services, illustrating the global reach of the Islamic deen.

Jizyah
A tax levied on Non-Muslims under Islamic rule, as commanded in Quran 9:29. Symbolizes submission and second-class status.

Justice
Justice according to Islamic doctrine consists in applying Allah's law as revealed. It is therefore inseparable from Sharia.

Kafir
A derogatory classification in Islamic doctrine for one who rejects, denies, or conceals the truth of Islam. Derived from the Arabic root *k-f-r*, which occurs more than 500 times in the Quran in its various forms, Kafirs are repeatedly condemned and described as deserving punishment, including in the hereafter. The classification also carries legal and social consequences under Sharia, distinguishing Kafirs from Muslims

in rights, obligations, and status. They are the 'worst of creatures... (Quran 98:6)

Koran (see also Quran)

Liberate/Liberation
In Islamic doctrine, to liberate a people or territory means to free them from man-made laws and bring them under the authority of Allah's law (sharia). The classic example is the conquest of Mecca in 630 CE, which Islamic sources describe as a liberation from idolatry and jahiliyyah (the period of ignorance). The goal is not political independence or national self-determination in the modern sense, but the establishment of Islamic governance. Contemporary calls to "liberate" territories are frequently rooted in this doctrinal meaning rather than secular notions of freedom.

Loyalty
In Islamic doctrine, allegiance is owed first to Allah, Mohammed, and the Ummah. Loyalty is owed to believers, while disassociation is required from unbelievers. See Wala' wa'l-Bara'.

Madrassa
An Islamic school that teaches the Quran, hadith, Arabic, and Sharia, including detailed rules governing personal behaviour and hygiene.

Martyrdom (Shaheed)
Islamic sources promise Paradise to those who die while fighting in the path of Allah (jihad), making martyrdom the clearest assurance of salvation. Suicide is prohibited in Islam, but those who die while performing jihad are not considered to have committed suicide.

Masjid
Arabic word for mosque, meaning "place of prostration." In Islam, a masjid is not only a site for worship but also a centre for teaching, rulings, communications, and sometimes political or military activity. While many are established as permanent religious endowments (waqf), it isn't a requirement.

Mercy
One of Allah's principal attributes. In Islamic doctrine, mercy is exercised according to Allah's will and justice as revealed in the Quran. Among the 99 Names of Allah are Ar-Rahman (The Most Merciful), as well as harsher names such as The Avenger, The Humiliator, and The Bringer of Harm.

Millah
The religious community or way associated with a particular prophet, especially the Millah of Abraham. The term appears about 15 times in the Quran. It is distinct from deen, which is used about 100 times in the Quran. Islam does not describe itself as a millah; the Quran uses deen for the comprehensive civilizational system established through Mohammed extending from governance and law to worship and personal conduct.

Mohammed
The founder of the Islamic deen (together with Allah as its ultimate source). He is described in the Quran as an excellent pattern for believers (Quran 33:21). The Quran instructs Muslims to follow his example in over 40 verses (some counts reach 89). He was a preacher, statesman, judge, legislator, military commander, and leader of jihad. The supreme human authority in Islam. His words, actions, and approvals (the Sunnah), together with the Quran, constitute the primary sources of Sharia and establish the binding precedent by which Muslims are expected to live.

Mosque
More than a place of worship. Traditionally, the mosque serves as the religious, educational, judicial, political, and social centre of the Muslim community. Mohammed's mosque in Medina also functioned as the headquarters of the first Islamic state.

Naskh (see Abrogation)

Oppressor / Oppression

In Islamic usage, includes those who resist Allah's authority or oppose Islam, rather than referring only to oppression in the modern Western sense of denying individual rights or liberty. Quran 2:193 commands fighting until fitnah ends and the din is for Allah, permitting hostility thereafter only against "the oppressors."

Ordained Way. See Sharia. (Quran 45:18.)

Paradise (Jannah)
The eternal reward promised by Allah to believers. Throughout the Quran and hadith, Paradise is promised for numerous prescribed acts of obedience, including prayer, building mosques, spending in the cause of Allah, participation in jihad, martyrdom. The promise of Paradise serves as a recurring incentive for conduct prescribed by the deen.

Peace
In Islamic doctrine, peace is the condition that results from submission to Allah and obedience to His ordained way. It is not simply the absence of conflict.

Personal Autonomy
In modern Western thought, individuals are generally regarded as free to make personal choices provided they do not unlawfully harm others. In Islamic doctrine, personal

autonomy exists within the limits prescribed by Allah and Sharia. Individual preference does not override divine command. (Quran 33:36)

Quran
The holy book of Islam, believed by Muslims to be the literal word of Allah, revealed to Mohammed. Divided into 114 surahs (chapters) and over 6,000 ayat (verses).

Religion
In modern Western usage, a system of personal belief and worship separate from civil government. This definition differs fundamentally from the Islamic concept of Islam as a deen.

Revelation
In Islam, the direct and literal word of Allah communicated to Mohammed through the angel Jibril (Gabriel). The Quran is regarded as the final, complete, and unalterable revelation, superseding all previous revelations where they differ.

Right
Consistent with the teachings of Islam. 'Enforcing the Right and Forbidding the Wrong' is an Islamic communal obligation.

Right Hand Possesses (Ma Malakat Aymanukum)
An Islamic expression referring to persons taken as slaves or captives. The phrase appears numerous times in the Quran and hadith establishing the basis for slavery, concubinage, and the legal rights and obligations of slave owners.

Sharia
The ordained way prescribed by Allah (Quran 45:18). The legal framework derived primarily from the Quran and the Sunnah of Mohammed. Where these sources do not provide an explicit ruling, Islamic jurists apply consensus (ijma') and jurisprudence (fiqh) to determine the law. Sharia governs all aspects of Muslim life and society, including worship, personal conduct, family life,

commerce, finance, criminal law, governance, and relations with Non-Muslims. Under Sharia, every human action is classified as obligatory, recommended, permissible, disliked, or forbidden (Reliance of the Traveller c2.1-5). In this book, the terms Sharia and Islamic law are used interchangeably.

Sira

Biographies of Mohammed's life. The earliest and most influential is Sirat Rasul Allah by Ibn Ishaq (d. 767), available in English as The Life of Muhammad, translated by A. Guillaume. The Sira provides the historical context for the Quran and hadith and is widely used to understand Mohammed's life, military campaigns, and the development of the early Muslim community.

Sunnah

The example, practices, judgments, and approvals of Mohammed that serve as a primary source of Islamic law alongside the Quran.

Surah (See Naskh)

A chapter of the Quran. The Quran consists of 114 surahs of varying length, ordered roughly from longest to shortest rather than chronologically. This obscures its parallel with Mohammed's life. Earlier verses from Mecca are intolerant but not violent; that changes after the migration to Medina, with later verses often superseding earlier ones (Quran 2:106). (plural: Surahs)

Tafsir

Scholarly commentary explaining the meaning of the Quran. Classical tafsir works, such as those of Ibn Kathir and al-Tabari, form an essential part of traditional Islamic interpretation.

Taqiyya

Doctrinal permission to lie or deceive when necessary to achieve a permissible goal under Islamic law. This includes protecting Islam, avoiding harm, reconciling parties such as a spouse, or securing advantage. Lying is not inherently sinful if the purpose is sanctioned and benefits Islam. There are many doctrinally affirmed variations such as tauriya - ambiguous speech to give a misleading impression, kitman – omitting information.

Tawhid
The absolute oneness of Allah. The central doctrine of Islam from which all other aspects of the deen derive

Terror
Fear inspired in an opponent. Mohammed said, "I have been made victorious with terror..." (Sahih al-Bukhari 2977). In practice, this includes legal and social mechanisms that punish criticism or non-conformity. For example, Saudi Arabia's counter-terrorism law criminalizes "calling for atheist thought in any form or calling into question the fundamentals of the Islamic religion," a definition so broad it can be applied to almost any dissent.

Terrorism
A term whose meaning depends on the legal system applying it. In some Islamic jurisdictions, anti-terrorism laws extend beyond acts of violence to include speech or conduct considered contrary to Islam or offensive to Allah, Mohammed, Sharia, or the Islamic state.

Truth
According to Islamic doctrine, truth is that which has been revealed by Allah. The Quran is regarded as the final and perfect revelation, and Mohammed as the final prophet whose example is binding. Claims that contradict this revelation are, by definition, regarded as false regardless of their source.

Ulama
A body of Islamic scholars recognised for their expertise in the Quran, hadith, and Sharia.

Ummah
The global community of Muslims. The Ummah is the organizing unit of the Islamic deen – a transnational community bound by a common source of authority, a common body of doctrine, a common legal framework (Sharia), common religious obligations (including the requirement of Arabic for prayer and recitation of the Quran), and a common obligation of loyalty among believers. It is not defined by nationality, ethnicity, or political boundaries, but functions as a nation without borders whose objectives are global (Quran 13:41, 21:44).

Wala wal-bara (Loyalty and Enmity)
A core doctrine in Islam requiring Muslims to show loyalty (wala) to Allah, Mohammed, and fellow Muslims, and to disavow (bara) Non-Muslims and all un-Islamic beliefs and practices. This loyalty includes love, support, and allegiance; enmity includes disapproval, separation, and enmity. The doctrine underpins Islamic social and political separation from Non-Muslims and is based on verses such as Quran 48:29 and Quran 60:4.

Wrong
Inconsistent with the teachings of Islam. 'Enforcing the Right and Forbidding the Wrong' is an Islamic communal obligation.

Zakat
The obligatory alms tax prescribed by Sharia and an individual pillar of Islam. The Quran specifies eight categories of recipients (Quran 9:60), including those "in the cause of Allah."

THE QUESTION THE WEST NEVER ASKED

An Orientation for the Reader

For centuries, Western scholars, diplomats, merchants, missionaries, adventurers and politicians have attempted to explain Islam to their own societies. Many worked diligently and in good faith, often under difficult circumstances and with limited access to original sources. Others approached the subject through the lens of their own religious and political traditions. The result was a body of scholarship that profoundly shaped Western understanding.

Yet one idea, repeated so frequently that it eventually became unquestioned, proved more consequential than all the others: Islam came to be classified as a religion.

That single classification shaped diplomacy, immigration policy, constitutional law, education, journalism, human rights, foreign affairs, intelligence analysis and public discourse throughout the Western world. Entire legal frameworks were constructed upon it, as politicians, judges and academics proceeded on the belief that the classification itself was accurate. This book begins with a different question: What did Mohammed actually establish?

If he founded simply another religion, then classifying Islam as a religion was correct and the discussion ends there. If, however, he established something fundamentally different – a comprehensive civilizational system that regulates every aspect of life – then the consequences of that misunderstanding have been immense. That question deserves to be answered before anything else.

Timeline of Mohammed's Life

Year	Event	Reference
570	Born in Mecca	Sira – Ibn Ishaq
610	Began preaching Islam	Quran 96:1–5
622	Migrated to Medina (Hijra)	Quran 8:72, Sira
623	Jihad begins – raids on Meccan caravans	Quran 2:190
630	Conquest of Mecca	Quran 9:28–29, Ibn Kathir
632	Died in Medina	Bukhari 3053, Sira

Mohammed's Role

Western readers tend to imagine Mohammed as fulfilling a role broadly comparable to that of the founders of other major religions. That assumption is understandable, but incomplete. Mohammed was certainly a preacher. He claimed to receive divine revelation, called people to submit to Allah, and proclaimed himself the final prophet. Yet he was also far more than that. He became a legislator, judge, military commander, diplomat, head of state, tax collector and supreme legal authority. His decisions governed not only worship, but warfare, commerce, inheritance, marriage, criminal justice, taxation, diplomacy and relations with non-Muslims.

These different roles are not incidental to understanding Islam. They are central to it. Unlike most religious founders, Mohammed united political, legal, military and religious authority in a single office. That authority did not end with his death. It continues through the legal framework known as Sharia, derived from the Quran and the binding example (Sunnah) of Mohammed himself.

- Quran 45:18 "We placed you upon a Sharia..."

Mecca and Medina

The first thirteen years of Mohammed's mission were spent in Mecca, where his movement remained relatively small and politically weak. Everything changed following his migration to Medina in AD 622. There Mohammed ceased to function merely as a preacher and became the ruler of an emerging state. During the remaining ten years of his life he established a legal order, commanded and fought in military expeditions, entered into and dissolved treaties, judged disputes, imposed taxation and directed the expansion of his community throughout Arabia.

- Quran 9:33, 48:28, 61:9 "...that He may make it prevail over all other deen."

The significance of Medina cannot be overstated. It marks the transition from proclamation to governance, from preaching to political authority, from private belief and practice to public law and order, the beginning of the Islamic calendar, and the adoption of Jihad as a means of expansion. Eight years later, Mohammed returned to Mecca at the head of a victorious army. After taking control of the city, he personally struck the approximately 360 idols in and around the Kaaba while reciting, "Truth has come and falsehood has vanished" (Quran 17:81). Their destruction ended the Kaaba's role as a centre for Arabia's diverse religious traditions and established it as the exclusive sanctuary of Islam. From that time onward, non-Muslims were excluded from the sacred precinct.

Within little more than a century of Mohammed's death, Muslim armies had expanded from Arabia across the Middle East, North Africa, Persia, and into Europe and the Indian subcontinent. The remarkable speed of that expansion reflected not simply military success but the establishment of an enduring legal and political system.

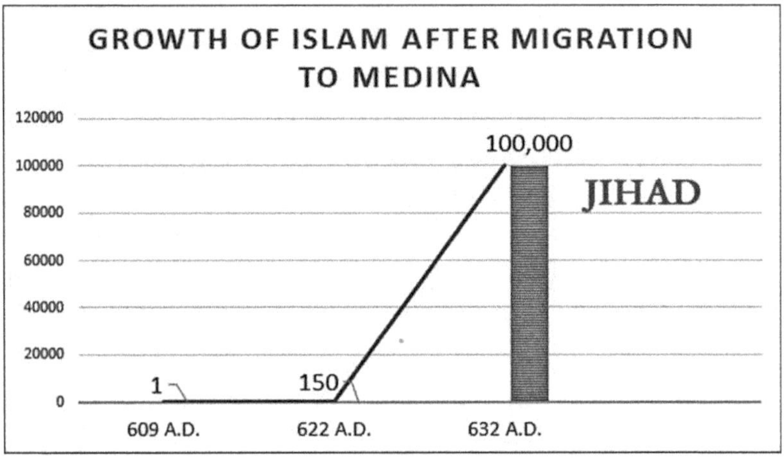

The Islamic calendar begins in 622 A.D. Jihad is adopted as a means of conquest. By 750 A.D. expanded to include Spain.

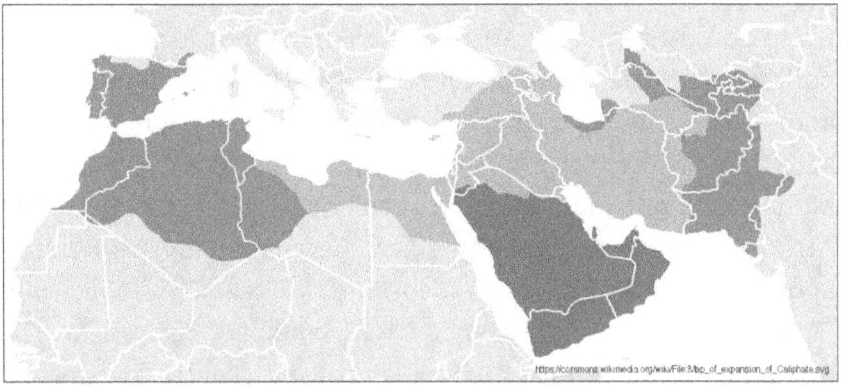

Expansion of the caliphate, 622–750 CE: Muhammad, 622–632 CE; Rashidun caliphate, 632–661 CE; Umayyad caliphate, 661–750 CE

The Sources of Authority

Islamic law is derived primarily from the Quran and the Sunnah. The Quran is believed to contain the literal words of Allah as revealed to Mohammed. The Hadith records Mohammed's words, actions, and approvals. Together these form the Sunnah, the normative example Muslims are expected to follow. Where these sources do not provide an explicit ruling, Muslim jurists rely on legal interpretation and scholarly consensus. The practical expression of these sources is known as Sharia.

Unlike modern legislation, Sharia is not regarded as human law subject to revision by elected governments. Its highest authorities are understood to be divinely revealed or permanently established through the example of Mohammed himself. That distinction is essential to understanding why the misclassification of Islam has been so consequential.

A System, Not Simply a Faith

Western societies naturally understand religion as something concerned primarily with worship, personal belief and moral guidance. Islam certainly contains all of these elements. Its foundational sources, however, also regulate government, courts, criminal justice, military conduct, taxation, personal hygiene, commercial transactions, family law, inheritance, international relations and the legal status of Muslims and non-Muslims alike. For Muslims, these are not separate spheres of life but expressions of the same revealed order.

Every comprehensive legal system must also define who belongs to the community it rules and how those outside that community are to be treated. Islamic jurisprudence is no exception. The Quran distinguishes consistently between believers and unbelievers. Those who reject Islam are referred to throughout the Quran as Kafirs, a term that appears more than 500 times. More than half of the Quran is devoted, directly or indirectly, to defining these unbelievers, explaining what they have done wrong, and prescribing how they are to be regarded, treated, or punished. This division has legal consequences.

Sharia assigns rights, obligations and legal status according to these classifications. Muslims and Kafirs are treated very differently within the traditional framework of Sharia.

Closely connected to these distinctions is the doctrine known as Wala wal-bara (Loyalty and Enmity). Rooted in Quran 48:29 and reinforced by the example of Mohammed, this principle has long shaped Islamic understandings of communal identity, allegiance and disassociation from non-Muslims. These concepts have no close equivalent within the constitutional traditions of liberal democracies, which presume equal citizenship under a common law regardless of creed.

This comprehensive legal, political and social order is referred to throughout the Quran by a word that has traditionally been translated into English as religion.

The Arabic word is Deen.

Why Translation Matters

Translations do not merely convert words from one language into another. They shape the concepts through which entire civilizations understand one another. When deen became consistently translated as religion, Western readers naturally interpreted Islam through the only category familiar to them. Churches replaced legal systems in the imagination. Worship took the place of governance. Personal faith displaced public authority.

Over time this misunderstanding became institutionalized as governments, courts, universities and international organizations built policies upon a classification that few had ever examined.

The consequences extend far beyond language. If Islam is simply another religion, then Western legal systems have largely responded appropriately. If deen instead denotes a comprehensive civilizational order encompassing law, social organization and political authority, then much of the modern West has spent centuries accommodating something fundamentally different from what it believed it was protecting.

The Doctrine is Unambiguous:

- Slavery is permitted in Quran 4:3, 4:24, 23:5–6, 33:50, and 70:29–30.
- Unbelievers are described as unclean in Quran 9:28.
- Women are required to veil in Quran 24:31 and 33:59.
- Blame for abuse of unveiled women is placed on the women themselves in Ibn Kathir's tafsir on 33:59.
- Non-Muslims are characterized as "less than livestock" in Quran 7:179 and as "the worst of creatures" in Quran 8:55 and 98:6.

It took only a few decades for Islam to conquer vast and diverse territories across the Middle East, North Africa, and Spain. Full conversion of populations took longer, but once Islamic authority was established, life for non-Muslims became progressively more difficult until conversion or permanent subordination as dhimmis became the only sustainable options. The pattern is consistent: where Islam holds power, the space for non-Muslims steadily contracts – in rights, status, opportunities, and safety.

What matters is that the legal and doctrinal framework that justified conquest and subjugation remains fully active today. This is the foundation on which the deen was built and through which it continues to expand.

"The believers are only the ones who have believed in
Allah and His Messenger, and then doubt not but strive
with their properties and their lives
in the cause of Allah.

It is those who are the truthful."

— Quran 49:15

PART I: CAUSE

For generations, English-speaking scholars, translators, dictionaries, encyclopedias, and public institutions have described Islam using concepts familiar to the West. In the process, vital distinctions were lost. A deen became a religion. Zakat became charity. Binding legal precedent became mere "history."

The chapters that follow examine how these misunderstandings took root, how they became embedded in English scholarship and policy, the consequences that have followed, and what correcting them requires.

Without these answers, the non-Islamic world will continue its descent, steadily falling to an entity that it cannot identify or resist.

1. The Deen Fallacy

Western societies generally assume that all civilizations understand themselves in broadly similar ways. We naturally interpret unfamiliar cultures through concepts that make sense within our own historical experience. What we call a religion is expected to concern matters of personal belief and worship. Law belongs to the state. Politics belongs to elected governments. Commerce, education, and family life occupy their own separate spheres. This division has become so familiar that many people assume it to be universal.

It is not.

While the West has consistently interpreted Islam through the category of religion, Islam's own foundational sources describe it as something much broader: a deen – a comprehensive order regulating worship, law, politics, commerce, family life, and society itself. This misclassification is not a matter of semantics. It has shaped more than a century of public policy, education, diplomacy, immigration, human rights, and constitutional debate.

The remarkable aspect of this misunderstanding is that the primary sources have always existed and have been remarkably well preserved. The Quran, the example of Mohammed, the canonical hadith collections, the classical biographies, the recognised commentaries, and the legal manuals have long described the Islamic deen in terms that differ fundamentally from the Western concept of religion.

Until recently, however, these sources remained largely inaccessible to the average person. For most of history, even obtaining a Quran in a language one could read was difficult, and collections of hadith, classical biographies, tafsir, and legal manuals were the domain of academics and religious specialists. As a result, public understanding of Islam has almost always been mediated through politicians, journalists, religious leaders, advocacy organizations, and self-appointed experts – many of whom describe Islam in terms that its own foundational texts do not.

Four examples illustrate the point.

- "Of the 99 names of Allah, none stand for force and violence... The fight against terrorism is not a confrontation against any religion." (Narendra Modi at the World Sufi Forum)
- "Peace is a core value in Islam, which is a religion of peace, which strengthens the values of peace, tolerance and coexistence." (Mohammed bin Abdulkarim Al-Issa – Leader of the Muslim World League)

- "Authentic Islam and the proper reading of the Quran are opposed to every form of violence." (Pope Francis, Evangelii Gaudium, 2013)
- "Islam is a religion which, like all the great religions, is a religion of peace and charity in the authentic sense of the term, which has nothing to do with the criminal expression that nothing can justify, that of the terrorists." (Jacques Chirac, Algiers, 2001)

Each of these statements was made by an influential public figure. Each presents Islam as fundamentally peaceful and compatible with modern pluralistic society. Yet none of them address the most basic question upon which any serious inquiry should begin: What do the Islamic sources themselves say?

Contrary to the statements above, the 99 names of Allah include the Avenger, All-Subduer, Giver of Death, Bringer of Harm, The Humiliator, The Owner of Dominion, and Possessor of Retribution. Exhortations to hostility and violence are found throughout the foundational texts:

- "Muhammad is the Messenger of Allah; and those with him are forceful against the disbelievers, merciful among themselves." (Quran 48:29)
- "And fight them until there is no fitnah and [until] the deen, all of it, is for Allah." (Quran 8:39)

Relying on the primary Islamic sources is surprisingly uncommon in public discussion. This book takes the opposite approach. Wherever possible, conclusions will be drawn from Islam's own authoritative sources – the Quran, the example of Mohammed, the canonical hadith collections, the classical biographies, the recognised commentaries, and the legal manuals that together define the deen.

Questions of law, governance, commerce, warfare, treaties, family life, and the ordering of society concern Muslims and non-Muslims alike. They are therefore not solely matters of private belief but of public consequence.

Muslims are routinely taught that Islam is not merely a religion. Islamic school curricula repeatedly explain that Islam is a deen (Aziz; Emerick 2000). One curriculum defines it as:

- "Deen, in fact, denotes a system of beliefs, a code of life. It does not merely signify the spiritual fulfilment of the individual. It means all matters pertaining to a way of life for it encompasses religion, law, trade, commerce, morality, politics, justice, foods, drinks, clothing – in fact, all aspects of life relating to people's thought or actions."

It goes on to describe Sharia:

- "Sharee'ah literally means a clear path which we must follow as we toil on towards the Creator whom we will eventually meet. In its fullest sense, the Sharee'ah virtually is the 'deen', which is often inadequately translated as religion. 'deen' literally means 'way of life', 'following' or 'the way'."

Classical Arabic sources associate deen with obedience, submission, judgment, authority, governance, requital, and an all encompassing system of life lived under a higher authority. Quranic usage reinforces this broader meaning. deen is used in connection with legislation, enforcement, reward and punishment, social order, political authority, and the system Allah intends to prevail over all others. The dominion verses – Quran 9:33, 48:28, and 61:9 – all use the word deen, not religion, creed, or church.

- Quran 61:9 "It is He who sent His Messenger with guidance and the deen of truth to manifest it over all deen, although those who associate others with Allah dislike it."

The distinction becomes even clearer when compared with another Quranic term: millah. Millah appears only a fraction as often as deen in the Quran. While deen occurs approximately one hundred times, millah appears roughly fifteen times. More importantly, the contexts differ. Millah is usually associated with a creed, tradition, inherited path, or communal religious identity, most commonly the "millah of Abraham." deen, by contrast, refers to the broader system of authority, obligation, conduct, judgment, law, and social order.

If Islam wished to present itself primarily as a creed or religious tradition, millah would have been the natural term. Instead, the Quran overwhelmingly describes Islam as a deen.

How then did the West arrive at a different conclusion?

Part of the answer lies in the history of Orientalism and the development of Islamic studies in Europe. Western scholars needed Arabic dictionaries and reference works to study Islamic texts. One of the most detailed and respected resources was Edward William Lane's Arabic-English Lexicon published between 1863 and 1893. Lane's work is thorough and does record the broader classical meanings of deen – including obedience, submissiveness, authority, judgment, and requital – but it is dense, difficult to navigate, and was never widely accessible to most students or general readers. It still isn't.

Instead, more practical and easier-to-use dictionaries became standard in universities. Chief among these was Hans Wehr's Arabic-English Dictionary, which gained widespread popularity because it was designed for reading modern Arabic. The original

German was published in 1952, the English translation in 1961. Wehr's entry for deen is limited to "religion," with no reference to its wider classical meanings.

Traditional Muslim scholars, by contrast, continued to rely on classical Arabic sources such as Lisān al-ʿArab, Tāj al-ʿArūs, and other authoritative lexicons, which preserve the full range of meanings of deen rather than reducing it to the Western category of "religion." Conversely, the Darussalam English-Arabic Romanized dictionary defines deen simply as "religion." The word "Romanized" in the title itself signals that the work is intended for non-Muslim readers rather than for native users of the classical Arabic sources.

But dictionaries were not the only influence. Marmaduke Pickthall's The Meaning of the Glorious Quran (1930) remains one of the most widely read English translations of the Quran, particularly among non-Muslims and new converts. Pickthall's was the first translation by a native English-speaking Muslim, which gave it immediate standing that earlier non-Muslim versions lacked. Contemporary reviewers, both Muslim and Western, praised its accuracy and English style; the Times Literary Supplement called it a literary masterpiece. It remained the preferred English version for many English-speaking Muslims through the middle decades of the twentieth century and has seen more than 200 reprints as of 2022.

His translation is discussed here at some length because of its lasting contribution both to the mistranslation of key terms and to a disarmingly favourable presentation of Islam. Since Mohammed is not merely a historical figure but the decisive precedent for sharia, an incomplete or softened account of his life leaves readers with an incomplete understanding of Islamic law itself.

Pickthall was not a detached academic observer. A British convert to Islam, he presented his work as a sincere effort to make the Quran accessible to English readers. But he also served the Nizam of Hyderabad and approached the Quran as a believing Muslim and admirer of Mohammed. His translation, introductions, and footnotes deserve examination not merely as scholarship, but as influential interpretations that helped shape the Western understanding of Islam.

Throughout the book, Pickthall's translation and commentary reveal a consistent apologetic approach that softens difficult aspects of Islamic doctrine and historical precedent while obscuring important distinctions in Quranic terminology. One of the most significant problems in Pickthall's work is his decision to translate both millah and deen as "religion." This is not a minor linguistic choice. He should have realized the broader meaning deen carries in the Quran.

By collapsing these distinct terms into the single English word "religion," and by consistently presenting Mohammed and the doctrine in a positive light, Pickthall helped make possible the later treatment of Islam as a private belief entitled to the legal protections of religion, while its political and legal dimensions remained largely unexamined.

In his introduction to the Medinan chapters of the Quran, Pickthall writes that after the migration to Medina (the Hijrah) Mohammed "was no longer simply a preacher; he was now the ruler of a State." While factually correct, the tone presents this transformation as a natural and positive development. In his account of the Meccan years he portrays Mohammed as a steadfast preacher facing unprovoked hostility, and the Quraysh as the aggressors who mocked, persecuted, and finally ostracised him. He does not pause over the fact that the Quraysh repeatedly sought compromise – offering to accept

Mohammed's religion if their gods could remain as intercessors, even offering to make him king – or that a society which already housed hundreds of idols was not, by nature, closed to new claims. Nor does he treat the later shift to political and military leadership in Medina as problematic, a change that many of Mohammed's own followers initially resisted. Several passages in the Quran itself indicate that fighting, even in self-defence, was difficult for many early Muslims to accept.

- Jihad (holy fighting in Allah's Cause) is ordained for you (Muslims) though you dislike it, and it may be that you dislike a thing which is good for you and that you like a thing which is bad for you. Allah knows but you do not know. (Quran 2:216)

Pickthall's commentary on military expeditions and his treatment of Jewish tribes is similar. When describing the expulsion of the Banu Nadir, he states that the Prophet "was obliged to take punitive action against some of them." He makes no mention of the scale of the action or the confiscation of their property. Likewise, in his introduction to Surah 33 (chapter), he refers to the treatment of the Banu Qurayza after the Battle of the Trench but omits the number of men executed (between six and nine hundred) and the enslavement of the women and children. These events are presented as unfortunate necessities rather than as part of a pattern of political consolidation through force – the expansion of a civilization, not a religion.

The selective approach is perhaps most clearly seen in what he chooses not to explain. His footnotes describe Zakat simply as a tax collected from the wealthy and distributed to the poor. He makes no mention of its doctrinally mandated use for acquiring influence or funding warfare in perpetuity even though this is explicit in Quran 9:60. A use that is characteristic of a civilization not a mere "millah" (religion). Nor does he note the

Quran's repeated calls for "goodly loans" to Allah and His cause (for example, Quran 2:245 and 57:11), or find it remarkable that an entire chapter (Surah 8) is devoted to the collection and distribution of booty obtained through caravan raids and military expeditions.

Pickthall's clear admiration for Mohammed and contribution to historiography is evident in his introduction to Surah 66. He writes, "Having set a great example of monogamic marriage, the Prophet was to set a great example of polygamic marriage." He records the tradition that verses 1–4 may refer to the incident in which Mohammed was found having sexual relations with Mary the Copt in the house and on the bed of his wife Hafsa, concluding that the wives were "presuming on his status," and accepts that Allah made the relationship lawful (al-Tabari tafsir). While extolling Mohammed's kindness, he does note the later temporary separation from his wives but does not mention the explicit threat of divorce and replacement with better wives if they continued to cause trouble came by way of revelation (Quran 66:5). Nor does he note that revelations frequently paralleled Mohammed's personal circumstances in ways that even his young wife Aisha remarked upon when she said, "I see that your Lord hastens to satisfy your desires" (Bukhari 4788).

His introduction to Chapter 17 describes Mohammed's Night Journey as a purely spiritual experience to the Temple of Jerusalem even though the word Jerusalem does not appear in the original Quran at all and no temple stood in Jerusalem at that time. Islamic sources themselves record disagreement about whether the Night Journey was physical or spiritual; Aisha is reported to have said that Mohammed's body never left the bed and that only his spirit travelled. Pickthall does not engage with the consequential political implications later attached to it whereby Islam claims Jerusalem as its own holy city. Nor does he mention the tradition in which Mohammed reportedly encountered Zaynab, wife of his adopted son Zayd, in Paradise as "a damsel with dark red lips" who greatly pleased him (Ibn Ishaq 265, 270).

In his note on Quran 33:37 Pickthall presents Mohammed's subsequent marriage to Zaynab bint Jahsh as a deliberate social reform: Mohammed arranged the original match to break down caste pride and later married her himself only to abolish the pagan Arab custom of treating adopted sons as real sons. Yet a full millennium earlier al-Tabari recorded that Mohammed went to Zayd's house, found Zaynab lightly clad, and admiration for her entered his heart; Zayd then divorced her and a revelation immediately permitted the new marriage (al-Tabari 1460-62). The same revelation abolished the legal status of adoption as previously practiced (Quran 33:37, 33:40), a change that remains in force to the present day.

The overall effect is to portray Mohammed as a man of exceptional moral character whose actions, however unusual for a religious figure, were always justified.

Throughout the work, difficult aspects of Islamic history and doctrine – such as the execution of prisoners, the treatment of non-Muslims, and the development of political authority – are either minimised or presented in ways that make them more palatable to a Western audience.

Pickthall was not unique in this approach. Many early Western converts and translators of the Quran sought to present Islam in a way that would be respectable to European readers and not offend Islamic scholars. However, because his translation was long regarded as one of the most reliable and scholarly available in English, its apologetic character and use of the word religion whether it was consistent with the Arabic understanding of the word or not, has had a lasting influence. Generations of readers have encountered the Quran through Pickthall's lens – one that consistently minimizes the political and legal dimensions of deen and presents early Islamic history in a more favourable way than the sources themselves support.

Even the greatest Orientalists of the nineteenth century accepted an inherited translation without subjecting it to sustained conceptual analysis. Aloys Sprenger was highly critical of the traditional Islamic sources and wrote extensively on Mohammed and early Islam, yet no discussion has been identified in his principal works arguing that the Arabic word deen is misleadingly translated into English as "religion." Like most nineteenth-century Orientalists, he accepted the conventional rendering. Theodor Nöldeke was one of the foremost philologists of his generation and paid meticulous attention to Quranic language in Geschichte des Qorāns. Although he examined many Arabic terms in detail, he does not appear to have argued that deen is inadequately translated as "religion." Like most scholars of his era, he generally employed the conventional translation without discussing the conceptual distinction.

The result was subtle but profound. Western institutions gradually interpreted Islamic terminology through Western categories. Religion became the most convenient – albeit inadequate – translation for deen, even though neither the Quran nor Islamic scholarship confines deen to the sphere that Western societies normally associate with religion. Once adopted by Western scholars, the classification was repeated by dictionaries, encyclopedias, academics, governments, courts, and the media until it acquired the appearance of settled fact. As a result, cohort after cohort of students and scholars have absorbed a dangerously inadequate definition of deen as religion and continue to defend that position without ever realizing how limited it is compared to classical usage.

This problem has been compounded by Islam's longstanding use of Judeo-Christian terminology when communicating with non-Muslims. Terms such as Abraham, Moses, Jesus, revelation, prophets, scripture, truth, faith, and religion all appear familiar to Western audiences. Yet familiarity does not establish equivalence. Islamic doctrine recasts these figures, concepts, and narratives to reflect the authority, law, and objectives of the deen rather than the original Biblical narratives from which they are drawn. Similar vocabulary often conceals profound differences in meaning.

2. Creedism: A Word We Don't Use Enough

The Ebenezer Baptist Church in Occoquan, Virginia – founded in the 1800s by a former slave with deep African-American roots – is now Masjid Al-Hussain. The town's creedist mayor, Earnie Porta, personally asked the mosque leaders to broadcast the adhan publicly. He believed it would be "something good for people in the town of Occoquan to hear... a good cultural experience."

Church bells do not proclaim doctrine. They do not tell listeners that Christianity is superior, that Jesus is the final prophet, or that everyone should convert. Historically, bells have served practical functions such as marking the time, calling congregants to worship, or announcing civic events.

The adhan, by contrast, is a spoken declaration of Islamic belief. It includes doctrinal affirmations such as "Allah is the greatest," "I bear witness that there is no god but Allah," "I bear witness that Mohammed is the Messenger of Allah," "Come to prayer," and "Come to success." This is creed, not merely sound. These are words that the entire community is now expected to hear, whether they wish to or not.

English does have a word for prejudice, discrimination, unequal treatment, or institutional preference based on creed: Creedism, alternatively spelled Credism. Derived from the Latin credere ("to believe"), it belongs alongside words such as creed, credible, credence, and credential. Yet despite its usefulness, it remains almost entirely absent from public discourse.

We readily recognize racism, sexism, ageism, and antisemitism, but when individuals or institutions discriminate, accommodate, privilege, or disadvantage others on the basis of creed, we seldom have the language to identify it. Most people are not even aware of the term "creedism," and lacking the vocabulary, they are unable to correctly name what is happening or speak out against it. As a result, creedism often passes without comment, or is attributed to something else, even when practised openly. Policies and practices that would be immediately condemned if based on race or sex frequently escape scrutiny when the distinction rests instead on creed.

When a creed is structurally hostile to those outside it, the refusal to collect or publish data by belief is itself a form of creedism. It removes the most informative variable from public view and leaves the effects of the doctrine without a name.

Changing the Conversation, One Word at a Time

Creedism is prejudice, discrimination, unequal treatment, punishment, or abuse arising from classifications based on creed or ideology. A person who engages in or supports such discrimination is a **creedist**. Unlike racism, creedism does not require the practitioner to hold personal animus. It arises wherever institutions or individuals adopt, enforce, or defer to distinctions created by an ideology, regardless of whether they themselves subscribe to it.

Creedism is not unique to Islam. Any organization that classifies people or distributes benefits primarily on the basis of creed engages in creedism. The constitutional implications, however, depend upon the nature of the creed itself. A creed whose observance is confined to voluntary religious practice presents different constitutional considerations from one that claims legal authority over society or teaches the supremacy of its own legal system.

In a recent example, a 13-year-old Muslim boy in Germany stated: "Since the majority of Germans are non-Muslims, then they are infidels. With the exception of the Arabs who live here.

The Germans are obliged to welcome us because they are our servants." (X video, July 2026)

The statement that non-Muslims are "our servants" is consistent with the Islamic doctrine of dhimmitude, derived principally from Quran 9:29 and elaborated in the Pact of Umar and subsequent works of Islamic jurisprudence. That verse instructs Muslims to fight those who do not believe "until they pay the jizyah willingly while they are humbled."

The boy's remark is a clear expression of creedism. At thirteen, he is already a creedist.

Islam classifies humanity first and foremost according to belief. The primary division is between the believer and the unbeliever. Classical Islamic jurisprudence constructs rights, obligations, loyalties, and legal relationships upon this distinction. Believers are described as "merciful among themselves" and "forceful against the disbelievers" (Quran 48:29). Those who reject Islam are characterized as "the worst of creatures" while Muslims are described as the "best of creatures." (Quran 98:6-7)

The same principle of deliberate opposition appears in ordinary practice. Mohammed instructed his followers: "The Jews and the Christians do not dye their hair, so be different from them." (Bukhari 3462) And: "Do not greet the Jews and the Christians before they greet you and when you meet any one of them on the roads force him to go to the narrowest part of it." (Muslim 2167a) The separation is not accidental. It is required, and it is meant to be enforced.

- Reliance of the Traveller o22.12 "The judge treats two litigants impartially, seating both in places of equal honor, attending to each, and so forth, unless one is a non-Muslim, in which case he gives the Muslim a better seat."

Believing women are instructed to distinguish themselves through dress so they may be recognised and treated according to Islamic standards of modesty and safety. These classifications are foundational. They also shape behaviour – whether they are Muslim or not – toward women who do not conform to the required standards of dress. Subjecting women to harassment or violence for failing to veil in accordance with Quran 33:59 is creedist behaviour.

When people are selected for advantage because they are believers, or excluded, pressured, or treated differently because they are unbelievers, describing the behaviour as racism is inaccurate. The operative distinction is not ancestry or appearance. It is creed. The behaviour is creedist.

Creedism does not only operate against those outside the belief. It also structures relationships and imposes restrictions within the believing community. Women appearing before Sharia courts, or young children required to wear full coverings that severely restrict movement and breathing, are subject to classifications and obligations derived from the same doctrinal framework. The distinction remains creed-based: different rules, expectations, and degrees of autonomy apply depending on one's status within the deen.

Classical Islamic law reflects this hierarchy by assigning different legal values to human life according to their status. In Reliance of the Traveller, a Classic Manual of Islamic Sacred Law (o4.9), it states:

- The indemnity for the death or injury of a woman is one-half the indemnity paid for a man. The indemnity paid for a Jew or Christian is one-third of the indemnity paid for a Muslim. The indemnity paid for a Zoroastrian is one-fifteenth of that of a Muslim. When a miscarriage results from someone having struck the stomach of a

> pregnant woman (or other part of her), or when someone frightens her resulting in a miscarriage, the indemnity for the fetus is a male or female slave worth one-twentieth of the indemnity payable for killing the fetus's father, or one-tenth that of its mother.

What makes creedism distinctive is that it can be practised by people who do not follow the creed from which the classification originates. Teachers, police officers, judges, university administrators, journalists, politicians, and corporations may enforce or accommodate doctrinal distinctions without believing the doctrine themselves. They become agents of creedism by accepting, institutionalising, or giving legal effect to categories they did not create.

When a U.K. police officer arrests a non-Muslim for burning a Quran or for describing Mohammed as a pedophile, that is creedism in action. When a public school removes pork from its menu to placate a creed, or an employer converts an employee gym into an Islamic prayer room, or a government office installs foot-washing facilities for wudu at public expense, that too is creedism in action.

Calling it By Its Name

The source of the discrimination remains the ideology. The practitioner may belong to any belief system, or to none. The effect, however, is the same: individuals are treated differently because of classifications derived from creed-based doctrine rather than from neutral, constitutional, or universal principles.

This pattern has been difficult for its victims and opponents to address precisely because the term creedism is not well known. Until recent times and the rise of Sharia-based demands upon Western society, the need for such a term was not widely recognized. That situation has now changed, and the language must evolve with it.

Although creedism is an established English word with a dictionary entry, it has remained largely absent from public discourse. Without a commonly used term, the phenomenon has stayed largely unexamined – or denied altogether, as though that which lacks a word cannot exist. The first step toward addressing it is to call it by its correct name.

Only then can we apply the same standard of scrutiny to creed-based distinctions that we already apply to those based on race or sex. Only then can creed-based discrimination be properly held to account.

3. How the West Was Taught to Misunderstand Islam

Ideas rarely become accepted by accident. They are transmitted through education, translation, scholarship, diplomacy, political necessity, and repetition. Once established, they become so familiar that few people think to question them. The modern Western understanding of Islam is no exception.

The central argument of this book is that Islam consistently describes itself as a deen – a comprehensive system of submission and obedience governing every aspect of individual and collective life. A concept for which non-Muslims have had neither a comparable frame of reference nor the vocabulary to describe it. Instead, for centuries, the English-speaking world has overwhelmingly understood the Islamic deen through the far narrower concept of "religion."

The result has been generations of writers discussing Islam as a civilization while simultaneously describing it as a religion. This was the cumulative product of successive translators, travellers, diplomats, lexicographers, artists, academics, and public figures, each contributing to a framework that increasingly reflected Western interpretations rather than Islam's own self-description.

The consequences have been profound. Public policy, education, diplomacy, immigration, constitutional law, and interfaith dialogue have all been shaped by a classification that differs fundamentally from the one found in Islam's primary sources.

Creedism has also advanced through legal and institutional mechanisms oblivious to, or actively downplaying, its political and judicial character. Once Islam was accepted in the Western mind as simply another religion, its legal, political, and institutional claims came to be treated as matters of religious freedom rather than governance – progressively obscuring its civilizational character and the comprehensive nature of the deen.

The following sections trace some of the principal stages in that process. They examine the historical transmission of Islam into English, the development of Islamic continuity claims, and the paradox that, despite unprecedented access to primary Islamic sources, modern societies have clung to outdated assumptions rather than confronting the doctrine itself. Understanding how this came about is an essential step toward correcting it.

The Origins of a Misunderstanding

Islam presents itself as the final and complete restoration of the original monotheistic religion revealed to Abraham. According to Islamic doctrine, previous scriptures were corrupted over time, and the Quran was sent to correct and supersede them. This claim of continuity is central to Islam's legitimacy. However, when examined against historical and textual evidence, the foundation for this continuity appears remarkably thin.

For Islam to be a genuine continuation of the Abrahamic prophetic tradition, one would reasonably expect to find supporting evidence in at least three areas: a verifiable genealogical connection between Mohammed and Ishmael rather than Isaac, both sons of Abraham; clear Quranic emphasis on Ishmael's line as the primary channel of prophethood, and independent historical or manuscript evidence that earlier scriptures were corrupted in the way the Quran claims. None of these are supported by available evidence.

Traditional Islamic sources, including Ibn Ishaq and al-Tabari, trace Mohammed's ancestry back only as far as Adnan. Based on the traditional oral genealogy recorded in al-Tabari, Adnan would have lived around 30 B.C., leaving a gap of nearly two millennia between him and Ishmael.

Abraham – Ishmael (2000 ~ 1800 B.C.)

No oral or documented connection between Mohammed and Ishmael

Al Tabari Volume 6 (p.37) c.9th

"The genealogists do not differ concerning the descent of our Prophet Muhammad as far as Ma'add b. 'Adnan which is as I have expounded."

1. Adnān (30 BCE)
2. Ma'add
3. Muḍar
4. Ilyās
5. Mudrikah
6. Khuzaymah
7. Kinānah
8. al-Naḍr
9. Mālik
10. Fihr
11. Ghālib
12. Lu'ayy
13. Ka'b
14. Murrah
15. Kilāb
16. Quṣayy
17. 'Abd Manāf
18. Hāshim
19. 'Abd al-Muṭṭalib
20. 'Abd Allāh
21. **Muhammad (570 CE)**

* *Allowing 30 years per generation = 630 yrs from Mohammed to Adnan.*

Beyond Adnan, the genealogy becomes speculative and is not supported by historical records. There is no independently verifiable chain connecting Mohammed to Ishmael. Despite this, Islamic tradition asserts that Mohammed belongs to the prophetic line of Ishmael. This claim is not derived from the Quran itself, which provides no narrative development regarding Ishmael's descendants or any prophetic lineage stemming from him. Instead, the connection appears to have been constructed later to establish religious and political legitimacy.

The Quran's treatment of the sacrifice story further weakens the claim of continuity. In Surah 37 (As-Saffat), Abraham is commanded to sacrifice his son, yet the Quran does not name which son was intended. Immediately after this account, the text mentions Isaac by name. This sequencing is significant. If the Quran intended to establish Ishmael as the son of the covenant and the channel of future prophethood, one might expect clearer identification and greater emphasis on his role. Instead, the text remains ambiguous on this critical point while continuing to draw heavily on stories centered on Isaac's line.

A further problem arises from the Quran's extensive use of biblical stories. While claiming that previous scriptures were corrupted, the Quran repeatedly appropriates and modifies Biblical narratives involving prophets from Isaac's line. This creates a logical difficulty: if those earlier texts were unreliable, why does the new revelation depend so heavily on their content?

Claims of perfect preservation are also increasingly difficult to maintain. Researcher Daniel Alan Brubaker, who has examined early Quranic manuscripts extensively, has documented thousands of physical corrections in the surviving texts (Brubaker). This level of scribal activity in the earliest manuscripts challenges the traditional narrative of an unchanged, perfectly transmitted text from the time of Mohammed.

Islamic Claim	Required Evidence	Available Evidence	Assessment
Mohammed descends from Ishmael	Verifiable genealogical chain	Genealogy stops at Adnan	Not historically verifiable
Ishmael's line is the channel	Clear Quranic emphasis on Ishmael	None beyond Ishmael. Only Isaac's line.	Not demonstrated

Islamic Claim	Required Evidence	Available Evidence	Assessment
of prophethood			
Previous scriptures were corrupted	Manuscript evidence of systematic alteration	Biblical manuscripts show stability	Strongly contradicted
The Quran is perfectly preserved	Early manuscripts with no significant variation	Thousands of documented corrections (Brubaker)	Significantly weakened
Islam restores the original religion of Abraham	Historical or textual continuity	Reliance on significantly altered biblical stories	Logical tension

A common argument used in Islamic discourse and disputation is that if Islam were false, people would have rejected it (Chowdhury). The continued existence of Islam is therefore presented as evidence of its "truth" (see Glossary). The Quran itself, however, records a very different picture.

Far from being universally accepted, Mohammed's claims were met with widespread skepticism, mockery, and outright rejection – particularly from his own tribe, the Quraysh. The Quran repeatedly responds to accusations that Mohammed fabricated his revelations, was mad, had been taught by others, or was practising deception.

These accusations appear across numerous surahs and fall into several distinct categories. Their persistence, together with the defensive nature of many Quranic responses, suggests they were neither isolated nor trivial.

1. Accusations of Fabrication and Invention

One of the most common accusations recorded in the Quran is that Mohammed had invented the revelations himself. Critics claimed he had created the Quran by drawing on old stories or by deliberate fabrication. Examples include:

- Surah 25:4-5: "Those who disbelieve say, 'This is nothing but a lie he has invented, and other people have helped him with it.'... And they say, 'Tales of the ancients which he has had written down, and they are dictated to him morning and evening.'"
- Surah 46:8: "Or do they say, 'He has invented it'?"
- Surah 52:33: "Or do they say, 'He has made it up'?"
- Surah 38:7: "This is nothing but an invention!"
- Surah 10:38 and 11:13: The Quran challenges the critics to produce even one or ten surahs like it – an implicit response to the claim that Mohammed had composed it himself.

These accusations suggest that many of Mohammed's contemporaries viewed the Quran not as divine revelation, but as a human invention.

2. Accusations of Madness or Demonic Possession

Another frequent accusation was that Mohammed was mad (majnoon) or possessed by jinn. This claim appears in several places:

- Surah 15:6: "O you upon whom the Reminder has been sent down, indeed you are mad."
- Surah 23:25: "He is not but a man possessed..."
- Surah 26:27: "Indeed, your messenger who has been sent to you is mad."
- Surah 37:36: "Are we to leave our gods for a mad poet?"
- Surah 44:14: "...[He is] taught [by someone], mad."
- Surah 68:2 and 81:22: The Quran defensively states that Mohammed is not mad, indicating that this accusation was serious enough to require repeated rebuttal.

The repetition of this claim across different surahs suggests it was a persistent and damaging accusation during Mohammed's mission.

3. Accusations of Being Taught by Others

Some critics alleged that Mohammed was not receiving revelation from God, but was being taught by another human being:

- Surah 16:103: "And We certainly know that they say, 'It is only a human being who teaches him.'"
- Surah 44:14: The disbelievers describe him as "taught [by someone], mad."

These accusations imply that at least some people believed the content of the Quran originated from human sources rather than divine revelation.

4. Accusations of Being a Poet, Sorcerer, or Liar

Mohammed was also accused of being a poet, a sorcerer, or simply a liar:

- Surah 21:5: "Rather, they say, '[It is but] a mixture of false dreams; rather, he has invented it; rather, he is a poet.'"
- Surah 38:4: "And the disbelievers say, 'This is a magician and a liar.'"
- Surah 52:29-30: The disbelievers are recorded as calling him a poet awaiting misfortune.
- Surah 34:8: Accusations that he was lying about Allah.

These claims attacked both his character and the source of his message.

5. Broader Rejection and Demands for Proof

Beyond specific accusations, the Quran records general skepticism and demands for visible proof:

- Surah 25:7-8: Critics complained that he was just an ordinary man who "eats food and walks in the markets."
- Surah 17:90-93: They demanded miracles – such as causing a spring to gush from the ground, having a house of gold, or ascending into heaven – before they would believe.
- Surah 6:7: Even if an angel came down visibly, they said they would still not believe.

The Defensive Tone of the Quran

What is particularly notable is not only the existence of these accusations, but the defensive posture the Quran adopts in response to them. Many verses are framed as direct rebuttals to critics. The Quran repeatedly denies that Mohammed is mad, insists that the revelations are not invented, and challenges the disbelievers to produce something similar. This stands in contrast to the portrayal of Jesus in the Gospels. While Jesus faced opposition and was eventually rejected by the religious authorities, the Gospel accounts do not present him as spending significant time defending himself against accusations of fraud or madness. His focus remained on teaching through parables and instruction rather than constant self-vindication. The Quran's repeated defensive responses suggest that Mohammed operated in an environment of ongoing and serious skepticism.

This pattern of reasoning is not limited to the Quran. It continues in later Islamic and non-Islamic scholarship. In his tenth-century work on disputation, Risālat al-Ādāb fī ʿIlm al-Baḥth wa'l-Munāẓara, Aḥmad ibn Muṣṭafā Ṭāshkubrīzāde offers an argument for the Quran's inimitability that assumes the seventh-century Arabs recognized it as a serious linguistic challenge and failed to meet it. This work, still studied and translated today, overlooks the Quran's own record that many contemporaries rejected Mohammed's claims outright – not because they could not match its language, but because they considered them false from the beginning. It also passes over the significant resistance that continued after his death, most notably the Ridda Wars, in which tens of thousands who had assumed that Mohammed's death would mark the end of their subjugation were killed.

Sir William Muir observed even as early as the nineteenth century that the Abrahamic genealogy of Mohammed was artificially constructed to fit Jewish and Biblical narratives. He described it as filled with "strange anachronisms" and "plagiarisms from rabbinical lore," noting that many of these traditions were later inventions designed to align Arabian history with the Old Testament (Muir).

Ironically, after examining the Quran, Muir wrote that he could find no evidence that Mohammed himself doubted the authority or genuineness of the Old and New Testaments as they existed in his time. This conclusion is difficult to sustain. The Quran contains multiple passages accusing the Jews of hiding, distorting, or rewriting parts of their scripture. Muir's claim reveals more about the limits of nineteenth-century Western scholarship than it does about the Quranic text itself.

- Quran 2:75 - Some are accused of hearing Allah's word and deliberately altering it after understanding it.
- Quran 2:79 - "Woe to those who write the Book with their own hands" and then claim it is from Allah.
- Quran 3:78 - Some are accused of twisting scripture with their tongues.
- Quran 4:46 - Some are accused of distorting words from their proper places.
- Quran 5:13 - They are accused of changing words from their proper places and forgetting part of what they had been reminded of.
- Quran 5:15 - The People of the Book are accused of concealing much of what had been revealed.
- Quran 5:41 - Some are again accused of altering words after their proper places.

Islam's claim to represent the restored and final form of Abrahamic monotheism rests primarily on Islamic assertion rather than independent historical or textual demonstration. The absence of a verifiable genealogical link to Ishmael, the Quran's repeated reliance on the prophetic line descending through Isaac while identifying no prophetic descendants of Ishmael, the ambiguous treatment of the sacrifice narrative, the heavy dependence on Biblical material while simultaneously claiming its corruption, and the growing evidence of textual variation in early manuscripts all point to serious flaws in the continuity claim.

Without external corroboration, the case for Islam as the continuation of previous revelations ultimately depends on accepting Mohammed's testimony alone that he was receiving direct revelation from God. This is a matter of faith, not historical or factual verification.

Early Observers Were Under No Illusion

The earliest surviving descriptions of Mohammed's movement are striking in what they emphasise. They do not portray an isolated preacher concerned solely with private belief or personal spirituality. Rather, they describe an ambitious man, and a movement that, from its earliest days, combined claims of divine authority with political and military expansion.

During the three-year period between Mohammed's first revelation and the beginning of his public preaching, al-Ṭabarī preserves an early tradition in which Mohammed's mission is explicitly linked to future conquest. According to the account, Mohammed's uncle, al-ʿAbbās, explains to a visitor who witnessed Mohammed's unusual method of prayer outside the Kaaba that Mohammed claimed God had sent him and that "the treasures of Chosroes [Persia] and Caesar [Rome] would be given to him by conquest" (al-Ṭabarī 1162).

Non-Islamic accounts from this period are exceedingly rare. One of the earliest, the Doctrina Jacobi (c. 634–640), similarly portrays Mohammed not simply as a preacher but as a man associated with warfare. One witness dismisses him on the grounds that "prophets do not come armed with a sword," while another reports that there was "no truth to be found in the so-called prophet, only the shedding of men's blood," together with his claims that he possessed "the keys of paradise, which is incredible" (Hoyland).

Whether written by Muslim or non-Muslim observers, these early accounts describe a movement in which claims of prophethood were accompanied by conquest, booty, political authority, and the exercise of power.

Terminology describing Islam as a deen, rather than a religion, appears in the earliest surviving monumental inscription commissioned by the Islamic state. Completed in 691–692 under the Umayyad Caliph ʿAbd al-Malik, the Dome of the Rock prominently proclaims: "There is no god but God alone." It identifies "Muhammad [as] the Messenger of God," and declares, "Indeed, the deen with Allah is Islam" (Quran 3:19), and repeats the Quranic proclamation that God sent His Messenger "with the guidance and the deen of Truth, that He may cause it to prevail over every deen" (Quran 9:33; cf. 61:9). Rather than describing a private religion, the inscription publicly affirms the Quran's own concept of deen.

Centuries later, European rulers dealing directly with Islamic powers continued to recognise the political character of the system they faced, even when commercial and strategic interests led them to cooperate with it.

Pragmatism, Trade, and Selective Historical Memory

Although the Crusades remained a defining chapter in relations between Christendom and the Islamic world, in the 16th century Elizabeth I deliberately cultivated trade and diplomatic relations with the Ottoman Empire because she regarded it as politically and commercially advantageous.

This episode stands in contrast to the broader historical record. The Crusades themselves, which ended less than three centuries before Elizabeth's reign, are often remembered in isolation, while the far longer history of Islamic expansion receives little attention. Roughly two-thirds of Christendom had already been conquered by Arab and Muslim forces through successive campaigns of jihad long before the First Crusade was launched in 1095 (Ye'or 1996). The Crusades were not unprovoked aggressions but were called in response to centuries of Islamic conquest, accompanied by widespread slaughter, enslavement, and the persecution of Christian populations.

In her first letter to Sultan Murad III, Elizabeth nevertheless described herself as "the most invincible and most mighty defender of the Christian faith against all kinds of idolatries." This declaration did not prevent the beginning of a diplomatic and commercial relationship that would continue for seventeen years (Brotton).

Shortly before writing to Murad, Elizabeth had authorized the establishment of England's first joint-stock company, the Muscovy Company – a model later replicated in England's expansion into India and North America. With Spanish and Portuguese ports largely closed to English merchants, trade with the Ottoman Empire offered substantial economic and strategic advantages. English merchants exported cloth, imported luxury goods such as sugar (a fondness for which eventually blackened Elizabeth's teeth) and spices, and even supplied munitions to the Ottomans during their conflict with Spain.

Another significant omission from the popular narrative is the extensive trade in European slaves carried out by Muslim powers in North Africa and the Ottoman Empire, which continued for hundreds of years after the Crusades had ended. Throughout that period, European captives were taken in raids along the coasts of Italy, Spain, France, and Britain and sold in Islamic slave markets. This trade in Europeans continued long after the Atlantic slave trade had begun and was brought to an end as a large-scale enterprise only through sustained military and diplomatic pressure, much of it led by Britain in the nineteenth century.

The Enlightenment and Religious Toleration

Nearly a century later, another development would have profound consequences for the way Islam was eventually accommodated within Western law. In 1689, the English philosopher John Locke published A Letter Concerning Toleration, one of the most influential arguments for religious toleration and the separation of religious and civil authority. Locke argued that the proper concerns of government were civil interests - life, liberty, health and property - while a church was a voluntary association concerned with the salvation of souls. Religious authority, in his conception, therefore had no jurisdiction over those who did not belong to it. His ideas would contribute significantly to the development of religious liberty and the constitutional separation of church and state (Locke).

Locke did not exclude Muslims from this principle. He specifically argued that neither a "Pagan nor Mahometan, nor Jew" should be denied the civil rights of the commonwealth because of his religion. Yet the distinction upon which his argument rested contained an assumption that would later become enormously consequential: that what was being tolerated was religion - something distinguishable from the authority of the state. Locke defined a church as a voluntary society whose proper concern was salvation, not civil government. Islam had developed upon a very different foundation. Mohammed had been not only a preacher but a legislator, judge, military commander and head of state, while Sharia regulated matters that Locke assigned to the civil sphere.

Indeed, Locke himself recognized limits to toleration remarkably relevant to this point. He argued that toleration need not extend to doctrines contrary to the preservation of civil society, to religious bodies claiming domination over others, or to those whose religious allegiance placed them under an external jurisdiction. The difficulty was therefore not with the principle of toleration itself, but with classification. A constitutional principle designed to protect freedom of conscience and voluntary religious association would eventually be applied to Islam as though Islam fitted the category for which that protection had been devised. The distinction between religion and deen had still not been made.

Nineteenth-Century Witnesses

By the nineteenth century, British knowledge of Islam no longer depended solely on diplomats, merchants, or distant reports. Increasing numbers of travellers, linguists, historians, archaeologists, artists, and Orientalists spent years living in Islamic societies, observing them firsthand. They visited palaces, courts and the homes of the elite while the Ottoman slave trade, including the enslavement of Europeans and Africans, remained an accepted part of public life.

They encountered functioning legal systems, slave markets, harems, concubinage, eunuchs, Islamic courts, pilgrimage, commerce, and daily life under Sharia. They witnessed Islam operating not merely as a faith but as a civilization governed by its own legal and social order.

Edward William Lane lived for many years in Egypt. His Manners and Customs of the Modern Egyptians describes slavery, concubinage, harems, the legal status of women, Islamic courts, and many other aspects of Egyptian society with remarkable detail. Richard Francis Burton travelled extensively throughout the Islamic world, disguised himself as a Muslim in order to enter Mecca – a deception that would almost certainly have cost him his life had it been discovered – and wrote extensively about slavery, pilgrimage, Islamic law, concubinage, eunuchs, and everyday life. Marmaduke Pickthall likewise travelled widely throughout the Middle East before converting to Islam and later producing one of the most influential English translations of the Quran (Lane, Burton).

What is striking is not what these men observed, but how they described it. They witnessed societies in which law, family life, commerce, slavery, taxation, and political authority were all shaped by Sharia. Yet English scholarship continued to present Islam primarily as a religion, while treating many of these institutions as historical, cultural, or incidental rather than as integral expressions of the deen itself.

Their accounts reveal genuine scholarship and careful observation, yet they also reflect the perspective of their class and era. Many appear to have compartmentalised what they witnessed, and that would have been entirely understandable. European observers arrived with their own conceptual categories already established. Prayer, pilgrimage, mosques, fasting and the Quran were readily identified as religion, while courts, contracts, taxation, marriage law, commerce, slavery and the regulation of social life looked like civil law and custom. Europeans themselves lived under civil laws governing many of the same matters. There was therefore little reason for a traveller observing an Egyptian slave market, an Islamic court or a marriage contract to assume that these belonged to the same system as prayer. What was easily missed is what the word deen reveals. The line the observer drew between religion on one side and law and social order on the other was his own. It did not describe Islam.

Writing in 1845, Sophia Poole's The Englishwoman in Egypt describes white European slave girls, black eunuchs, harems, concubinage, slave markets, and the severe discipline imposed upon female slaves with matter-of-fact precision (Poole). At about the same time David Roberts spent almost a year in the Middle East compiling 272 watercolour sketches. He recorded mosques and pilgrimages as worship, and slave markets, governors and local custom as separate facts of the country. He saw both. He did not join them. These were contemporary observations by educated British witnesses living in Islamic society. Yet the significance of these institutions as expressions of a functioning deen, justified by irrevocable foundational doctrine, received remarkably little attention in the English understanding of Islam that developed at that time.

Some may simply have accepted Muslim explanations that such practices reflected local culture rather than Islamic doctrine. Others, owing to the unavailability of Islamic doctrine in English, may simply not have recognized the connection between creedist texts and practice. Still others clearly admired aspects of Islamic civilization despite institutions they regarded as objectionable, or wrote with particular audiences, patrons, or political realities in mind. Pickthall, as a convert, had the additional consideration of defending the deen he had embraced.

Whatever the reasons, the cumulative effect was the same. Western readers inherited descriptions of Islam that documented its institutions in considerable detail while continuing to classify the system itself as a religion.

Just as sixteenth-century English merchants and statesmen set aside religious objections when it served commercial interests, later governments and institutions have adopted similarly pragmatic approaches to Islam. The result has been policies that reflect immediate political advantage and administrative priorities more readily than careful consideration of the long-term constitutional implications.

From Elizabethan Pragmatism to Colonial Legal Structures

Centuries later, this pragmatism took a more permanent form in British colonial policy in India. Even though India had already spent centuries resisting Islamic domination, experienced as conquest, government, jizya and law rather than as a private faith, British administrators concluded that Islam was best understood as a religion - comparable to other faiths within a plural society. They institutionalised separate personal laws for Muslims through the Muslim Personal Law (Shariat) Application Act of 1937.

The arrangement reflected administrative convenience and political pragmatism rather than constitutional consistency. This was compounded after 1947 when later Indian governments chose to retain and even strengthen many of these arrangements rather than moving quickly toward a Uniform Civil Code.

This legislation preserved Islamic rules on marriage, divorce, inheritance, and family relations. The justification was familiar: religious freedom and the protection of minority rights required that Muslims be regulated by their own legal traditions in matters of personal status. What was not seriously examined was whether Islam functioned as a private religion in the Western sense, or whether it constituted a comprehensive system of expansion that included its own framework of law, authority, and social order.

The consequences of this decision remain visible today. Article 44 of the Indian Constitution directed the state to work toward a Uniform Civil Code, yet more than seventy-five years later this objective remains largely unrealized. Criminal and constitutional law apply equally to all citizens, but in significant areas of personal and family life, Islam continues to operate under different legal standards.

This arrangement has had lasting demographic and social effects. Muslim personal law, combined with higher fertility rates, has contributed to a steady increase in the Islamic share of India's population since partition – from roughly 9 percent in 1947 to approximately 15 percent today. At the same time, reports of temple desecrations, the kidnapping and forced conversions of Hindu girls, and communal violence continue to surface with regularity. These patterns are not new. As one Indian observer recently noted, Bharat (India) has been confronting Islamic expansion for roughly fourteen centuries, during which vast territories across the Indian subcontinent fell under successive Muslim dynasties, long before the partition of 1947 (personal communication).

What eventually became a British habit of writing Islamic personal law into the constitutional order was soon exported elsewhere. Nigeria's 1999 Constitution still provides for a Sharia Court of Appeal in any state that requires one and confines its core jurisdiction to "Islamic personal law" (ss. 275 and 277). Kenya's Constitution retains Kadhis' courts for Muslim personal status, marriage, divorce and inheritance (Art. 170), a colonial arrangement carried into independence. These clauses treat Islam as a creed entitled to its own courts, yet the courts apply a body of law. In Malaysia, Parti Islam Se-Malaysia (PAS) has said the same thing in plain words. Its president, Abdul Hadi Awang, has called for Islam in the Federal Constitution to be read as ad-din, not as "religion." The demand itself confirms what the colonial drafts already assumed in practice: the system being accommodated was never only worship.

Nor was this pattern confined to Britain.

A Parallel Process in France

France followed a closely parallel course, though its history reveals something particularly significant: the legal and political meaning of the word din had once been recognised.

In 1647 the French diplomat and orientalist André du Ryer published L'Alcoran de Mahomet, the first complete translation of the Quran directly from Arabic into a European vernacular. It became enormously influential and served as the basis for subsequent translations into English, Dutch, German and Russian (Du Ryer). The first English version, made from Du Ryer by Alexander Ross in 1649, retained the rendering of din as "Law" in the key dominion verses. Later modern translations, however, overwhelmingly shifted to "religion."

Du Ryer himself did not translate din uniformly. Significantly, however, in each of the three dominion verses (Quran 9:33, 48:28 and 61:9) he rendered din as loy (law). Where modern translations commonly present Mohammed as sent with the true "religion" so that it might prevail over every other "religion," Du Ryer gave the correct interpretation: Mohammed had been sent with the true law, which was to prevail over every other law.

- Quran 61:9: "il a envoyé ſon Prophete pour conduire le peuple au chemin de ſalut, pour luy enſeigner la verité de ſa loy, & pour la faire paroiſtre plus que les autres loix du monde contre la volonté des infidelles."

As Brent Nongbri has shown in *Before Religion*, this early choice better reflects the classical range of the term (custom, judgment, and obligatory prescriptions to which one must submit) than the later reduction to "religion" or "faith." The legal and comprehensive force of din was therefore visible to some of Europe's earliest translators of the Quran. The subsequent narrowing of the word to "religion" cannot be explained simply by an absence of knowledge.

A century and a half later, Napoleon Bonaparte demonstrated the political usefulness of presenting compatibility with Islam. When French forces invaded Egypt in 1798, his proclamation assured Egyptians that he had not come to destroy their religion and declared his respect for God, Mohammed and the Quran. The French original described the French as "true friends of the Muslims." The Arabic version, prepared by Napoleon's own orientalists, deliberately went further and told Egyptians that "the French are also true Muslims" (Nelson). Friendship was transformed into shared Islamic identity for the benefit of the occupied population. It was political pragmatism in unusually explicit form.

More than two centuries later, Canadian Prime Minister Mark Carney's 2026 declaration that "Muslim values are Canadian values" echoes the same political instinct under entirely different circumstances. The historical situations differ, but the mechanism is the same: political authority asserts compatibility with Islam without first defining the doctrines with which compatibility is being claimed.

In Algeria the same pragmatism became institutional structure. After the conquest began in 1830, France inherited a society long shaped by Islamic law and governance. Colonial authorities nevertheless reorganised it through familiar European categories. Islamic law was retained largely for personal status and inheritance, while other domains were placed under French law. At the same time an official *culte musulman* – Muslim worship – was constructed and supervised by the state (Surkis 2019). Islam was thus administratively classified as a *culte* (religion), even as a distinct body of Islamic law continued to operate. The existence of that separate law itself demonstrated that the system extended far beyond worship.

- "L'indigène musulman est français; néanmoins il continuera d'être régi par la loi musulmane." (Sénatus-consulte du 14 juillet 1865)

Britain and France therefore travelled different historical roads to a similar destination. In both cases, elements of Sharia were preserved while Islam itself was classified within the European category of religion.

The problem was not simply that European elites did not know. At times they plainly did. The deeper problem was that political convenience repeatedly proved more attractive than accurate classification.

That same pattern has now returned across Europe. In Britain, more than eighty-five Sharia councils currently operate, and decisions made under their authority have been granted legal recognition by the courts (House of Commons Library 2019). In France, the long colonial experiment of classifying Islam as a culte while retaining elements of Islamic personal law has left its own institutional legacy. The same problem now appears across Europe. In 2019 the Parliamentary Assembly of the Council of Europe noted that members of Muslim communities in member states, "sometimes voluntarily, often under considerable social pressure," accept "religious" jurisdiction in marital, inheritance and commercial matters, and expressed concern that such rulings discriminate against women.

The consequences of treating Islam as a religion rather than as a comprehensive deen – a parallel system of law and authority – are now being paid by the citizens these states exist to serve and protect. What began as short-term political convenience has become a long-term burden on the populations whose security and legal equality were subordinated to that convenience.

In an Age of Unlimited Knowledge – The Paradox

The problem of inherited ideas versus direct engagement with primary sources becomes even more striking in the present age. For most of human history, ignorance had an excuse. Books were rare. Languages presented formidable barriers. Travel was slow and sometimes dangerous. Manuscripts were scattered across monasteries, royal libraries, and private collections, accessible only to a small number of scholars, clergy, diplomats, and government officials. Ordinary people relied upon intermediaries to interpret the world for them because they had little practical alternative.

That world has disappeared.

For the first time in history, ordinary citizens possess direct access to the foundational texts of one of the world's major civilizations. An English-speaking reader can consult multiple translations of the Quran, the major hadith collections, the biographies of Mohammed, the great works of tafsir, classical manuals of Islamic law, historical chronicles, academic studies, searchable databases, and vast digital libraries from almost anywhere in the world – a body of material still largely inaccessible in most other languages.

Information that once required years of travel and access to specialist collections is now available within seconds.

This transformation represents one of the most significant intellectual opportunities in human history, and with it a corresponding responsibility. The sources are available in a form that most of the world does not possess. Leaving them unread means failing to use the one clear view of the doctrine that is readily available, at the very moment when the English-speaking world is in a position to act on it and thereby offer a lead that other non-Islamic states can follow.

Yet it has produced an unexpected paradox. As access to information has expanded, the willingness to examine it directly has continued to diminish.

Rather than asking what the primary sources actually say, public discussion increasingly revolves around those considered qualified to interpret them. Attention shifts from evidence to authority, from documentation to credentials, and from verifiable sources to approved narratives. The question "What do the Islamic sources teach?" is replaced by another: "Who is permitted to speak about them?" Ironically, many of those who discuss Islam in contemporary Western society consult very little original material. Opinions proliferate while direct engagement with the evidence becomes increasingly uncommon.

That question matters because some of Islam's most significant objectives are neither hidden nor obscure.

The Quran states the objective of the deen with remarkable clarity. Three separate verses – Quran 9:33, 48:28, and 61:9 – declare that Allah sent Mohammed "with guidance and the deen of truth to make it prevail over all other deens." This objective is not presented as temporary, regional, or symbolic. It forms part of Islam's own description of itself and remains embedded within the primary sources.

Whether individual Muslims agree with this goal is beside the point. The point is that it exists, it is plainly stated, and it can be examined directly by anyone willing to read the sources.

QURAN 61:9

It is He who has sent His Messenger
with guidance and the ~~religion~~ ***deen*** of truth
to manifest it over all ~~religion~~ ***deen***,
although they who associate others with Allah dislike it.

Knowledge is Power

Islamic civilization has long understood the strategic value of knowledge. It acquired not only a thorough understanding of its own foundational texts but also the societies beyond its borders, recognising that diplomacy, commerce, treaties, and warfare required detailed knowledge of non-Muslim legal and political systems.

Many non-Muslims approach Islam in the opposite way. Instead of examining the primary sources themselves, they rely on personal experience, media reporting, or the assurances of those who identify as Muslims. More surprising still is the way contemporary Western institutions discourage direct engagement with those sources. Discussion is redirected away from doctrine and toward personalities. Questions about the reliability of primary sources become questions about the credentials of the person citing them. Criticism of ideas is recast as criticism of people.

A recent example illustrates the pattern. An Austrian newspaper criticized the establishment of a new advisory body on Islamic violence and related security concerns. Rather than considering the Islamic sources upon which the committee's concerns were based, the article concentrated on discrediting the individuals involved. Particular emphasis was placed on the absence of an "Islamic scholar," as though authoritative knowledge of Islamic doctrine should be restricted to those who practise it.

This represents a remarkable inversion of normal scholarly standards. Those who devote years to studying the primary texts but do not adhere to the doctrine are treated as inherently suspect, while those bound by the doctrine are presumed to be the only ones qualified to judge it. In almost no other field would such a standard be considered acceptable.

A Muslim participant on such a committee is not in a position to provide an objective review. Elements within the Ummah actively enforce the duty to "enjoin the right and forbid the wrong," that is, to uphold Sharia. Deviation or perceived criticism can bring social pressure, fatwas, or worse. Recent examples range from scholars who fear fatwas after critiquing Islamic finance to thousands of threats sent to non-Muslims merely for appearing in a "moderate Muslim" campaign (Saleem: Polis). The expectation of impartiality is therefore unrealistic.

Historical arguments are judged by the evidence supporting them, scientific claims by experiment and observation, and legal arguments by statute and precedent. The study of Islam should be no different.

This pattern reflects creedism in practice: the institutional treatment of Islam as a protected creed whose doctrines must not be subjected to the same level of scrutiny applied to other belief systems or political ideologies. The sources themselves remain available, yet public attention is diverted away from them. Knowledge is not only suppressed by destroying books or prohibiting access to texts. It is suppressed by encouraging people never to open them.

4. Education, Hybrid Warfare, Fatwas and Dawa

What Muslim Children Are Taught

One of the strongest tests of any translation is to compare it with the way the same concepts are taught to those expected to live by them. Islamic school texts provide precisely that opportunity. Across thousands of mosque schools, hundreds of full-time Islamic schools, and extensive home-schooling networks throughout the English speaking world, Islamic concepts are taught to Muslim children from an early age (Ellinger, 2026).

While Western audiences are told that Islam is a religion, zakat is charity, and Mohammed's military campaigns belong to history, Muslim children learn that Islam is a deen, that zakat is a legal obligation with prescribed recipients including jihad in all its forms, and that Mohammed's example is binding upon Muslims today and embodied in Sharia. These ideas are reinforced through repetition, ritual, memorization, group identity, and other established methods of conditioning.

This distinction extends well beyond terminology. While Islamic scholars devote their lives to the study of primary sources, the average Muslim student is introduced to Islam through approved curricula, teachers, and study guides in which the authority of Sharia is taken for granted, the establishment and expansion of Islam are presented as divinely ordained, and the examples of Mohammed and the early Muslim community provide the standard against which all conduct is measured – even so far as the position one assumes while sleeping. These ideas are presented as enduring principles.

The curriculum presents an overwhelmingly favourable picture of Islam. Sharia is described as the ideal legal system, Islamic human rights are portrayed as superior to those developed in the West, and Islamic history is framed primarily through examples of justice, compassion, and social harmony toward the Ummah. At the same time, Mohammed's military conquests and the expansion of Islam through violent jihad and the demand for tribute are glorified.

In spite of Mohammed's capture and enslavement of thousands of people, both directly and through the imposition of dhimmitude and tribute, students are told that Islam abolished slavery long ago. He is presented only as freeing slaves, never as buying, selling, or trading them – which he did. At the same time they are taught that his example forms part of the unchanging basis of Sharia, and that Sharia supersedes every other system of law. The two claims cannot both be true.

Such contradictions are not uncommon throughout the curriculum. Topics that could complicate an uncritical narrative such – the killing of apostates, the legal status of non-Muslims under Sharia, hudud punishments, the beheading of between 600-900 Jews who opposed Mohammed in Medina, the continuing Sharia-based endorsement of slavery and concubinage, receive little or no attention.

Students are correctly instructed that Islam is a deen, but the significance of that concept is not explored in its entirety. Consequently, many Muslims may understand the terminology of the deen without appreciating what it means in practice and fail to see that the Sharia applied in Taliban courts and the Sharia administered by councils and tribunals in non-Islamic countries derive from the same legal tradition and operate along the same continuum.

The result is an education that emphasizes the benefits of the Islamic order while giving comparatively little attention to aspects of Sharia that modern Western readers find difficult, thereby cultivating a worldview that sits uneasily alongside the principles of constitutional rule.

Children are growing up within an intellectual environment that differs markedly from the values of the surrounding Western society, even while enjoying the freedoms and legal protections provided by that society.

Western authorities that might be expected to exercise oversight express no concern that the basic principles of Islamic law stand in direct contradiction to the democratic principles of the countries in which the children are being raised. Some go further and publicly assert that Islamic values are national values even though Sharia is not consistent with their constitutions.

This refusal to confront the conflict is an expression of creedism. Because Islam is classified as a religion rather than as a comprehensive political and legal order, Western institutions treat its educational content as a matter of private belief rather than as the transmission of an alternative legal system. A system that is committed to "enjoining what is right and forbidding what is wrong" according to Sharia – a communal obligation upon all Muslims.

That same system imposes another communal obligation: jihad. In traditional Islamic law, jihad in the way of Allah is a communal obligation (fard kifayah). No other belief system imposes a perpetually financed and divinely mandated communal duty of warfare that remains binding until the end of time.

Reliance of the Traveller – a Classic Manual of Islamic Sacred Law (o9.1) states that jihad is a communal obligation. "When enough people perform it to successfully accomplish it, it is no longer obligatory upon others." However, "If none of those concerned perform jihad, and it does not happen at all, then everyone who is aware that it is obligatory is guilty of sin, if there was a possibility of having performed it."

If Western institutions accept that aspects of Sharia must be accommodated because they form part of a protected religion, the same rationale would have to extend to jihad. It is not an optional extra. It is a communal obligation within the same system.

But as the children are taught, Islam is not a religion; it is a deen, and therein lies the difference.

From Classroom to Leadership

By the time many Muslim students leave secondary school, they have spent more than a decade studying Islam through curricula that consistently present it as a deen. They have learned that Mohammed's example establishes the model for conduct, that Sharia is divinely revealed, and that its authority extends into every sphere of life.

Few young people are likely to challenge the authority of trusted teachers, approved textbooks, and a curriculum presented as divine truth. Belief in Mohammed as the final messenger, and in the Quran as the only uncorrupted revelation, is an article of faith. Previous scriptures are described as having been altered, leaving the Quran as the sole reliable source. True belief requires not only acceptance, but active submission to Sharia and obedience to the law of Allah and His Messenger. This point is emphasized repeatedly.

The curriculum also establishes clear boundaries regarding sources of authority. Students are frequently encouraged to rely upon the Quran, the Sunnah, recommended Scholars, and Islamic educational institutions when seeking guidance. External criticism is portrayed as the product of misinterpretation, prejudice, or ignorance. Classical sources that contain less favourable material, such as Ibn Ishaq's biography of Mohammed, are not assigned. Students are instead directed to modern authors including Sayyid Qutb, Mawdudi, and others. Having been taught that Islam is a complete and perfect deen, and that kafirs – unbelievers – are the "worst of creatures," students naturally come to regard any competing view with caution.

- "O you who believe! Obey Allah and obey the Messenger and those in authority among you..." (Quran 4:59)

From Leadership to Influence

Education, however, is only the first stage. The formation of future leadership requires more than classroom instruction. It requires opportunity, networks, mentorship, and access to positions of influence. In many Western countries, that process is supported through scholarships, leadership programmes, charitable foundations, and professional development initiatives directed specifically toward young Muslims.

The Avicenna Foundation in the United Kingdom provides a useful case study. Its scholarships are offered exclusively to Muslim students and do considerably more than remove financial barriers to higher education. Successful applicants receive full tuition funding at the University of Cambridge, allowing them to study without student debt and reducing the financial burden on their families. They are supported by personal coaches and mentors, participate in annual retreats in Britain and overseas, and become part of an achievement-oriented network designed to foster long-term success. The programme also provides opportunities rarely available to most undergraduates, including access to a dedicated space in Westminster, exposure to high-level institutional environments, and opportunities to speak in the Houses of Parliament.

Taken together, these benefits do not simply support academic achievement; they cultivate confidence, professional networks, and early familiarity with the institutions through which public policy is shaped. Participants are encouraged to see themselves as future leaders capable of shaping British institutions.

Viewed in isolation, there is nothing remarkable about scholarships or mentoring. Universities, churches, charities, and professional organizations have long invested in promising young people, although few, if any, offer anything comparable to the breadth of opportunity provided by Avicenna. The distinction lies elsewhere. These programmes build leadership within a community whose formative education has already presented Sharia as the ideal legal and moral order and Mohammed's example as permanently normative and beyond reproach. The scholarship does not create that worldview; it assumes it and invests in those who already possess it.

The result is a continuous pathway from Islamic education to civic influence. Children are introduced to Islam as a comprehensive deen. That understanding is reinforced throughout their schooling. Leadership programmes then cultivate the confidence, qualifications, networks, and institutional access needed to carry those ideas into universities, the civil service, the legal profession, politics, journalism, education, and public administration. Each stage builds upon the one before it.

This is not neutral "uplift." It accelerates entry into the upper echelons of British civic and political life for a cohort selected explicitly owing to their belief system.

This is a clear example of creedism in practice. Leadership programmes are deliberately structured around deen identity, granting advantages and accelerated access to positions of influence on the basis of creed rather than merit or citizenship alone. The long-term consequences of facilitating such a programme are not considered.

This does not mean that every participant will seek the implementation of classical Sharia or reject the constitutional order of the country in which they live. Individuals differ greatly in their beliefs and aspirations. It does, however, raise a legitimate public question. When programmes intentionally cultivate future leaders drawn from a community whose foundational education teaches the superiority of Islamic divine law over human legislation and commands obedience, what principles will guide those leaders when the two come into conflict? That question deserves careful examination because the future of constitutional democracies ultimately depends upon the source of authority to which public officials believe they owe their highest allegiance.

When Hybrid Warfare Calls Itself A Religion

The formation of future leadership within a framework that presents Sharia as the ideal order raises a broader strategic question. What happens when an entity advances its objectives through coordinated activity across political, educational, economic, social, legal, demographic, and informational domains, yet describes itself not as a state or political movement, but as a religion?

In 2017, the Multinational Capability Development Campaign (MCDC), a consortium including Canada, the United States, the United Kingdom, Germany, the Netherlands, Norway, Finland, Denmark, Austria, Switzerland, Italy, and the European Union, published a report titled Understanding Hybrid Warfare. The report was intended to help governments recognize and respond to modern threats that no longer rely solely on conventional military force. Instead, it described hybrid warfare as:

- "the synchronized use of multiple instruments of power tailored to specific vulnerabilities across the full spectrum of societal functions to achieve synergistic effects."

The report identified political, military, economic, social, informational, and infrastructure vulnerabilities as potential targets. It explained that hybrid entities often operate through multiple fronts simultaneously, exploit ambiguity, remain below traditional detection thresholds, and create cumulative effects that become visible only after significant changes have already occurred.

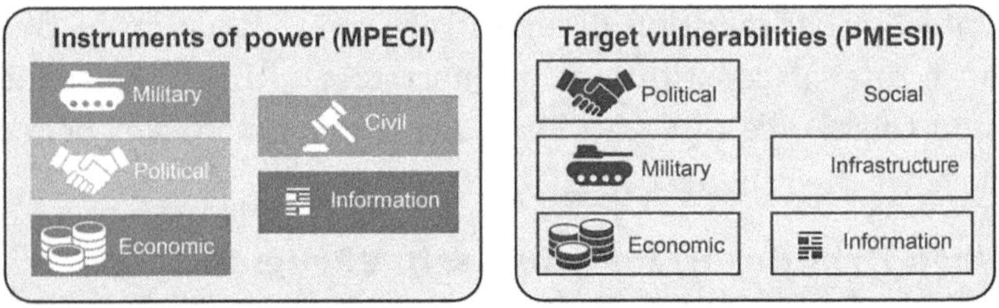

Figure 1.1 – MPECI instruments of power and PMESII target vulnerabilities

Five years later, the MCDC revisited many of the same themes in a report titled Multi-Domain Multinational Understanding. Although the project had expanded to include France, Spain, Poland, Sweden, Hungary, South Korea, Japan, Romania, and NATO, the report largely described the same phenomenon. What had changed most noticeably was the language. The plain-English term "hybrid warfare" had given way to expressions such as "multi-domain competition" and "multi-domain operations." Yet modern competitors are still described as pursuing advantage below the threshold of armed conflict, operating simultaneously across multiple domains, exploiting vulnerabilities within democratic societies, and generating cumulative effects through coordinated activity over time.

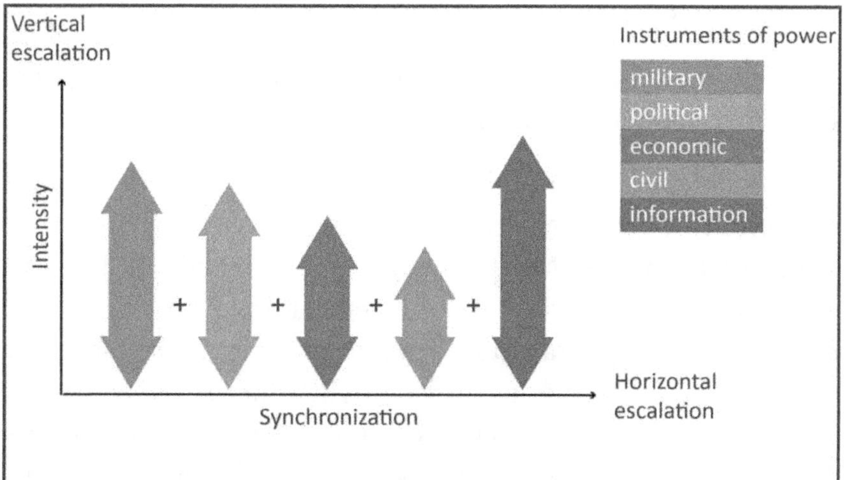

Figure 1 – Hybrid warfare escalation

An interesting question arises. What happens when an entity employs many of the same methods but describes itself not as a state, movement, or military organization, but as a religion?

The question becomes particularly relevant when examining Islam.

Western governments generally classify Islam as a religion, a designation that confers considerable privileges. Yet Islam describes itself as a deen, and Sharia is the practical implementation of that deen in law and society.

The MCDC framework evaluates entities according to what they do, not what they call themselves. If an entity advances simultaneously through political, economic, educational, social, legal, demographic, informational, and religious channels, the framework does not exempt it from analysis merely because it adopts a particular label.

The missing element in most Western analysis is the entity itself. Russia is recognized as an entity. Iran is recognized as an entity. Yet when examining Islam, Western governments, intelligence agencies, and security services focus on individual organizations, mosques, charities, schools, advocacy groups, businesses, migrants, or terrorist groups as though they were unrelated phenomena. Islam does not view them that way.

The organizing unit of Islam is the ummah – a transnational community bound by a common law, a common source of authority (Allah and Mohammed), a common body of doctrine, a common calendar, a common legal framework (Sharia), a common system of taxation, common religious obligations, a common language, and a common obligation of loyalty among believers. The ummah functions as a nation without borders. Its institutions may be local, but its identity, authority structure, and long-term objectives are global. A Grade 12 Islamic studies textbook puts the point plainly: "all historians declare that the amazing success of Islam in dominating the world lay in the astounding coherence or sense of unity in the group."

Through zakat, the obligatory tax levied on Muslims under Islamic law, resources are collected and redistributed according to categories established in Sharia. Classical authorities such as Reliance of the Traveller, major tafsirs, and Quran translations that include commentary such as Hilali-Khan identify categories that include support for jihad and the winning over of potential allies.

4.	**Those whose hearts need to be reconciled (*al-mu'allafatu quloobuhum*)** This includes people who have recently become Muslim. They also include the people whose evil acts can be prevented. They are also those who require to be given money to seek their support for Islam or to prevent them from opposition. They may be given *zakaat* to reconcile them by showing at first hand the caring nature of Islam.

Islamic school texts shown here teach children that zakat funds the propagation of Islam, disbelievers whose conversion to Islam is desired or whose opposition is to be restrained, and jihad. In modern terms, these functions correspond closely to influence operations and military operations. The ummah therefore possesses not only a common source of authority and law, but also a permanent mechanism for financing activities that advance its objectives.

> 7. **For the Cause of Allah (*fee Sabeelillaah*)**
> The seventh category where *zakaat* can be spent according to the Qur'an (9: 60) is spending in the way of Allah. This refers to *jihad*, or fighting for the sake of Allah. It means giving help to a struggle for making Islam supreme on earth. It is significant to realize that *jihad*, or striving, is not restricted to armed struggle only. It could also include writing, lecturing, and organizing work to support or defend Islam.

Some components progress through education, some through law, some through economics, some through politics, some through demographic growth, and some through violence. Islamic doctrine recognizes all of them as serving the interests of the same ummah.

These texts contain an extensive body of law covering political authority, legislation, courts, taxation, criminal penalties, warfare, relations with non-Muslims, and much more. Throughout history, Muslim rulers have implemented these principles through Sharia-based legal systems. In contemporary non-Islamic states, Islamic organizations routinely seek accommodation, recognition, exemptions, and influence within existing political structures.

Viewed objectively, the expansion of Islam presents characteristics that closely resemble the model described by MCDC. The difference is that the Islamic system predates the model by more than a millennium.

Consider the fronts identified in the report and compare them with well-known Islamic obligations and institutions.

Economic

The MCDC report identifies economic pressure as a major instrument of hybrid activity. Islam likewise advances through economic mechanisms. Halal certification systems, zakat networks, Islamic finance institutions, charitable foundations, waqf endowments, community funding structures, and the informal hawala system create a parallel economic ecosystem capable of operating across national boundaries and regulated in whole or in part by Sharia. The hawala system, in particular, is frequently used for money laundering and the transfer of funds outside formal regulatory oversight because it leaves almost no paper trail (El Qorchi; Maimbo; and Wilson 2003). These institutions are reinforced through lobbying efforts, foreign funding, and transnational networks of support.

Social

Islam places great emphasis on preserving the ummah, regulating marriage, defining group boundaries, encouraging loyalty to fellow Muslims, and maintaining distinct communal identities. Islamic schools, mosques, youth programs, charities, social organizations, and community institutions reinforce these bonds generation after generation. These relationships and obligations are established and maintained through Sharia. The Quran repeatedly warns adherents against befriending or forming a true alliance with those outside the ummah except as a precaution (Quran 3:28).

Informational

The report highlights information operations, influence, narrative management, and ambiguity. Islamic dawa serves precisely this function. Its purpose is persuasion, recruitment, image management, and expansion. Internally, the mosque functions as a communications and control centre. Islamic organizations devote enormous resources to shaping public understanding of Islam while simultaneously discouraging scrutiny of primary sources. Discussion is redirected from doctrine toward personalities, credentials, intentions, and accusations of prejudice.

Educational

Although not separated as an independent category in the MCDC framework, education operates across several of its domains simultaneously. Islamic schools transmit doctrine, reinforce identity, establish behavioral norms, create loyalty structures, and define relationships with non-Muslims. The process begins in early childhood and continues throughout life.

Beyond the classroom, educational institutions create networks of influence through credentials, professional recognition, academic partnerships, foreign funding, scholarships, and leadership development. Graduates acquire access to legal, political, educational, media, and governmental institutions while maintaining ties to transnational Islamic organizations and sources of authority. As these networks expand, they increasingly shape the institutions in which they operate, influencing hiring, policy, curriculum development, public discourse, and access to positions of authority.

Demographic

The report notes that hybrid entities exploit vulnerabilities and create long-term effects. Migration, settlement patterns, family formation, and community concentration all influence political representation, institutional influence, consumer markets, educational demand, and public policy. These changes occur gradually and often remain below public attention until their cumulative effects become significant. All are consistent with the preservation, growth, and strengthening of the ummah as prescribed by Sharia.

Legal

Perhaps most importantly, Islam advances through a comprehensive legal framework. The objective is not merely private belief. Islamic jurisprudence addresses virtually every aspect of human conduct. The MCDC report repeatedly warns that hybrid threats exploit vulnerabilities in legal, political, and institutional systems. Sharia constitutes precisely such a system of governance.

Today the legal dimension extends far beyond classical jurists. Thousands of Muslim lawyers, academics, advocacy organizations, and legal charities operate within Western legal systems. Using the language of constitutional rights, anti-discrimination law, human rights, and religious freedom, they pursue litigation and public policy objectives that align with the interests of the ummah.

For example, in 2017, the Council on American-Islamic Relations (CAIR) launched a mobile app assisting Muslims to report alleged incidents of discrimination instantly from their phones, virtually anywhere in the world. Users can submit complaints, identify the location, and request intervention – not only for personal experiences, but also for perceived bias in the media or on social platforms. These reports are then classified by CAIR as examples of "hate" and utilized as the basis for legal action or advocacy.

The legal dimension operates in two distinct but complementary ways. While Muslim lawyers and advocacy organizations work within Western legal systems, Islamic jurisprudence continually applies Sharia through its own legal mechanisms. The legal domain therefore operates simultaneously through Western legal institutions on the one hand, and through Islamic jurisprudence on the other.

One question naturally follows. If the Quran and the example of Mohammed cannot be altered, how, in addition to using Western court systems, does Islamic law exert its influence in the twenty-first century?

The answer is the fatwa.

A fatwa is an Islamic legal ruling issued by a qualified jurist applying the Quran, Sunnah, and Sharia to a particular question or circumstance. Unlike legislation enacted by governments or judgments issued by state courts, fatwas are produced continuously by qualified jurists throughout the Muslim world. Millions are issued each year on subjects ranging from personal conduct and family life to banking, insurance, investment, medicine, artificial intelligence, citizenship, elections, international law, migration, and jihad.

Location is largely irrelevant. The Islamic deen is organized around the Ummah, not the nation-state. A Muslim in London may seek guidance from a jurist in Cairo, Karachi, Riyadh, Jakarta, or elsewhere if he regards that jurist as authoritative. Today, many jurists answer questions through dedicated websites, online fatwa services, email, television programs, and social media, making Islamic legal guidance available almost instantaneously throughout the global Ummah.

- "The source of legal rulings for all the acts of those who are morally responsible is Allah Most Glorious." (*Reliance of the Traveller*, a1.2)

This is one of the principal mechanisms by which new circumstances are addressed without altering the deen's foundational authorities. The Quran is not rewritten. The

Sunnah is not revised. Instead, new questions are answered by applying the same primary sources to new situations. In this way, the deen remains both rooted in the seventh century and continuously applicable in the twenty-first.

This distinction is important. Western observers assume that ancient legal systems become historical relics unless they are extensively revised through legislation or judicial precedent. The Islamic deen operates differently. Its foundational authorities remain fixed, while their application is continually extended through jurisprudence. Far from being static, it is a living legal system capable of responding to technological, political, economic, and social change wherever Muslims reside.

Unlike a civil legal system, whose jurisdiction ends at national borders, the jurisdiction of the Islamic deen extends wherever members of the Ummah seek and accept its legal guidance.

Integrated Structures

The Islamic deen is self-perpetuating. Its schools educate the next generation. Zakat finances its activities (Quran 9:60). Sharia defines its communal obligations, including dawa, jihad, and the enforcement of Islamic law.

These obligations are not confined to Muslims alone. According to Islamic doctrine, Sharia is the only legitimate legal and moral system for all humanity. Non-Muslims are expected to live under it, either by conversion or as subordinate dhimmis. Islamic sources present Mohammed as a messenger sent to all mankind and Islam as a deen intended to achieve dominion over all others (Quran 9:33, 48:28, 61:9). Its institutions reinforce one another.

Individual Muslims may participate to varying degrees, but the system advances through its own internal incentives and structures.

Western leaders typically recognize warfare only when it is formally declared by a nation-state. For Islam, however, the Quran itself serves as that declaration. It commands warfare against non-Muslims until Islam prevails over all other ways of life.

This doctrinal reality is overlooked by those who expect conflict to follow the Western model of declared interstate war.

Cumulative Effects

The MCDC report makes an important observation. Hybrid activity often emerges from the synchronization of many independent actions that collectively generate effects greater than any individual component. The same principle applies to the ummah. No single mosque, school, charity, business, scholar, activist, or family changes society by itself. Yet together, they become greater than the sum of their parts.

Western governments have spent years developing frameworks to identify hybrid warfare conducted by states, militias, and political movements. Yet when it comes to Islam, authorities charged with protecting society from hybrid threats become reluctant to apply the same analysis.

History demonstrates that civilizations rarely collapse all at once. Their institutions are weakened gradually, one concession at a time, one exception at a time, one accommodation at a time, until the original framework no longer exists. Preserving constitutional government is not an academic exercise. It requires the courage to act, regardless of the label.

46. Acquiring and preparing force in all its forms is a religious obligation. It is the only way to prevent aggression by enemies against Muslim lands, protect holy sites, lives, property, and honor of Muslims, and prevent their displacement.
47. It is religiously forbidden, for a ruler as much as for a governed, to ask the resistance to lay down arms, due to the certain harms this causes vis-à-vis illusory gains. On the contrary, it is necessary to support the resistance by all means of strength.
48. Calling for the disarmament of the mujahidīn and depriving them of their means of defense constitutes treason against God, His Prophet, and the believers. It is a conspiracy against the Palestinian cause, an abandonment of the Muslim holy sites, and a victory served to their enemies.

Figure 1 Figure X. Excerpt from the Charter of the Scholars of the Ummah Concerning the Flood of al-Aqsa (June 2025), signed by over 500 Islamic scholars.

Dawa: The Invitation Before Submission

Among the various instruments through which Islam advances, one deserves particular attention because it operates primarily in the informational and influence domain: Dawa.

One of the most persistent misunderstandings in the West concerns the Islamic concept of dawa. It is commonly translated as "invitation" or "calling," leading many non-Muslims to assume that it is the Islamic equivalent of Christian evangelism or interfaith outreach. Government agencies, churches, universities, and civic organizations participate in dawa initiatives believing they are encouraging mutual understanding between communities. From the perspective of Islamic doctrine, however, dawa serves a different purpose.

The modern application of dawa extends well beyond formal outreach to adults. One of its most effective contemporary expressions targets non-Muslim children through schools. For many decades, Western secular public education specifically excluded confessional religious instruction in order to preserve state neutrality. In recent years, however, this principle has increasingly been relaxed. Programmes that include mosque visits, World Hijab Day activities, and similar initiatives are presented as opportunities for cultural enrichment, diversity, and inclusion rather than as forms of religious engagement. During these visits, children are warmly received, often invited to try on or gifted Islamic clothing such as the hijab, shown how Muslims pray, and introduced to Mohammed through carefully chosen narratives that present him in a kindly and beneficent light.

From the perspective of Islamic doctrine, however, such activities function as a form of early dawa. They create a positive emotional impression of Islam in young minds at an age when critical faculties are still developing. Children return home with a warm and sympathetic view of Islam, believing they have gained genuine insight into Islam and that it is merely a religion. What they do not realize is that this presentation is highly selective.

Topics such as the classical treatment of non-Muslims, the legal status of slaves and concubines, the capture and sale of women and children during Islamic conquests, or the doctrinal obligation to make the Islamic deen prevail over all others are never mentioned. The result is a form of psychological inoculation. When these same children later encounter criticism of Islamic doctrine, they are more likely to dismiss it as prejudice or misunderstanding because their earliest encounter was entirely delightful.

This approach aligns closely with the informational and influence operations described in hybrid warfare frameworks. When dawa is directed at non-Muslim children through schools and presented as harmless cultural education, it functions as a creedist instrument. It shapes future attitudes and loyalties while shielded from scrutiny by the very classification that allows it to operate.

It requires no coercion and generates little public resistance because it is presented as neutral cultural enrichment. Yet over time, it shapes the attitudes of future voters, journalists, teachers, civil servants, and political leaders – precisely the demographic that will determine how Western societies respond to the continued expansion of Islamic influence. In this sense, dawa directed at both Muslim and non-Muslim children through schools is not separate from hybrid activity; it is one of its most subtle and long-term instruments.

Within the Islamic deen, dawa is the invitation to accept Islam and submit to the authority of Allah. It is not an end in itself but the opening stage of a broader process established in the Quran, exemplified by Mohammed, and incorporated into classical Islamic jurisprudence. The invitation is extended first. If it is accepted, the objective is achieved peacefully. If it is rejected, Islamic law provides further alternatives, including submission through the payment of jizya or armed jihad. Sharia manuals such as Reliance of the Traveller require that the invitation be extended before military action, making dawa the first stage of Islamic expansion rather than a separate activity divorced from it.

The Western conception of dialogue differs fundamentally from the Islamic practice of dawa. Dialogue assumes two parties meeting as equals in search of mutual understanding. Dawa begins with the conviction that the truth has already been revealed completely through Allah and Mohammed. Its purpose is therefore not to discover truth together, but to invite others to accept the truth that has already been established. The objective is conversion, or at minimum acceptance of Islamic authority.

Mohammed's own career illustrates this pattern. Before military campaigns, invitations were commonly extended to rulers and communities calling upon them to embrace Islam. One of the best-known examples is his correspondence with the Byzantine emperor Heraclius, in which he quoted Quran 3:64:

- "Say: O People of the Scripture! Come to a word that is equitable between us and you: that we shall worship none but God..."

Read in isolation, the verse appears to be an appeal to common ground. Read in its historical context, it formed part of Mohammed's diplomatic invitation to accept Islam before further action followed. Classical commentators such as Ibn Kathir note that this verse was used in Mohammed's correspondence with Christian rulers and reflected his established method of extending dawa before political or military confrontation.

The same verse, Quran 3:64, was invoked more than thirteen centuries later in *A Common Word*, a 2007 letter from 138 Muslim scholars to Pope Benedict XVI and other Christian leaders. Although presented as an appeal to dialogue, it illustrates the continuing use of the same Quranic invitation in modern engagement with Christian leadership (Coughlin).

The encounter with the Christians of Najran in 631 followed a similar pattern. They declined to embrace Islam but accepted Islamic political authority through the payment of tribute. Later, after the revelation of Quran 9:29, the legal basis for such arrangements became explicit:

- "Fight those who do not believe in Allah... until they pay the jizya with willing submission and feel themselves subdued."

What had first appeared as practice was subsequently fixed as legal precedent within Islamic law. The invitation, the refusal, the payment of jizya, and the resulting subordinate status became part of the classical jurisprudence on relations between Muslims and non-Muslims.

Upon Mohammed's death the Jews and Christians of Arabia were later expelled. One of the instructions he left, recorded in Bukhari 3053, was: "Expel the pagans from the Arabian Peninsula, respect and give gifts to the foreign delegates as you have seen me dealing with them." The practice of using gifts to secure influence, already visible in his lifetime and reflected in the allocation of zakat "for those whose hearts are to be reconciled" (Quran 9:60), has continued ever since. The sequence he established became the model studied by later jurists.

For this reason, reducing dawa to "missionary work" or "interfaith dialogue" obscures its doctrinal role within the deen. It is not merely an invitation to discuss religious ideas. It is the opening phase of a legal and political process whose ultimate objective is the expansion of the deen under Islamic authority. Whether that objective is achieved through voluntary conversion, acceptance of subordinate status, or ultimately through force depends upon the circumstances, but the invitation itself remains the first step.

In contemporary Western societies, adult dawa rarely takes the form of direct theological debate alone. It is advanced through mosques, charitable organizations, universities, professional associations, social media, prisons, hospitals, workplaces, interfaith initiatives, community outreach programmes, and political advocacy. These activities are typically presented as humanitarian, educational, or cultural engagement. Viewed individually, many appear entirely benign. Collectively, however, they function as a distributed system of outreach through which Islamic beliefs, identity, influence, and institutional presence are progressively strengthened within both Muslim and non-Muslim communities (Siddiqi; Emerick 2010).

This historical model has never disappeared. It continues to shape contemporary Islamic outreach, although its presentation has adapted to Western audiences. Documents such as A Common Word Between Us and You, the Methodology of Dawah, and the Pocket Dawah Manual all present Islam in language designed to resonate with non-Muslim audiences while remaining firmly rooted in the classical objective of expansion. The methods have become more sophisticated; the doctrinal foundation remains unchanged.

PART II: CONSEQUENCE

Ideas have consequences. Once Islam was widely understood as a religion comparable to those of the West, public policy increasingly reflected that belief. Institutions, governments, courts, educators, and communities responded accordingly, without recognizing that many of the issues they faced arose from the practical application of a deen rather than the private observance of a religion.

The chapters that follow explore some of those consequences, illustrating how a mistaken classification has influenced public life, legal decisions, education, and the continuing relationship between Western societies and Islamic doctrine.

1. The Godless Governance of Islam

Islam is not what the West thinks it is. While it presents itself as a religion to gain unobstructed entry into secular legal and social frameworks, its goal is not spiritual growth or private belief. It is state control. Wherever Islam gains power, it rules through law, not faith. Iran is the most recent and extreme example of legislated creedism – the systematic privileging of one creed and the legal subordination of all others. In January 2026, the regime slaughtered an estimated 36,500 unarmed men, women, and children – using heavy machine guns and targeted headshots – to enforce obedience and suppress calls for its removal (Iran International).

- Quran 8:39 'And fight them until there is no fitnah and [until] the deen, all of it, is for Allah . And if they cease - then indeed, Allah is Seeing of what they do.'

The Cairo Declaration of Human Rights in Islam, adopted by Islamic states at the United Nations, identifies mankind as Allah's 'vicegerent' on earth – agents responsible for carrying out His commands. In Islamic doctrine, to "make war upon Allah" includes opposing, disbelieving, or obstructing the implementation of His will. Classical commentary, including Ibn Kathir on Quran 5:33, explicitly includes blocking roads among such acts.

Governance is not optional; it is an Islamic obligation codified as law. It requires submission, not devotion.

- Quran 2:30 'Behold, thy Lord said to the angels: "I will create a vicegerent [khalifah] on Earth." They said: "Wilt Thou place therein one who will make mischief therein and shed blood? - whilst we do celebrate Thy praises and glorify Thy holy (name)?" He said: "I know what ye know not.'

Islam Exploits a Universal Human Need – But Corrupts It

Faith is part of being human. From prehistoric times, people have reached for something higher – God, gods, nature, the unknown. This universal drive exists across cultures and centuries. It is spiritual, emotional, instinctive, and often transformative.

Islam takes this human impulse and corrupts it. It turns faith into a system of obedience, codifies belief into law, compels submission through fear, and replaces spiritual depth with carnal reward.

- Quran 9:111 'Indeed, Allah has purchased from the believers their lives and their properties [in exchange] for that they will have Paradise. They fight in the cause of Allah, so they kill and are killed.'
- Quran 56:17-23 'There will circulate among them young boys made eternal. With cups, and jugs, and a glass from the flowing wine. And fruit of what they select. And the

> meat of fowl, from whatever they desire. No headache will they have therefrom, nor will they be intoxicated... And (there will be) Houris (fair females) with wide, lovely eyes. The likenesses of pearls well-protected.'

The Quranic paradise is not divine – it is hedonistic. It promises virgins, wine, silk garments, and endless physical pleasure, with Mohammed's example reinforcing that vision. The highest virtue in Islam is not contemplation, mercy, or spiritual enlightenment – it is jihad: fighting and dying in the path of Allah.

- "Know that Paradise is under the shades of swords." (Bukhari 2818)
- "A man came to Allah's Messenger and said, 'Instruct me as to such a deed as equals Jihad (in reward).' Mohammed replied, 'I do not find such a deed.'" (Bukhari 2785).
- "I would love to be martyred in Allah's Cause and come to life and then get, martyred and then come to life and then get martyred and then get resurrected and then get martyred." (Bukhari 7226)

This is not a deen of personal conviction. It is a contract. For those who fight and die in its cause – or remain out of fear of being killed if they leave, or in the West at least, shunned – it is conscription. That Muslims profess belief in God is not proof of Islam's truth. It is proof of humanity's nature. Even atheists seek meaning – through ideology, cause, or tribe. But in Islam, that longing is exploited and perverted – as were the texts of established and ancestral beliefs, reinterpreted to serve its own claims. What Muslims experience as faith is not because of Islam – but in spite of it.

- Mohammed said: 'I have made successful through terror' (Bukhari 2977)

- Quran 4:80 'He who obeys the Messenger [Mohammed], has obeyed Allah'
- Quran 45:18 'Then We put you, [O Muhammad], upon a Sharia ...'

The ordained way is Sharia – a system of governance, not faith. Belief is the one thing Islam does not compel. Once it has power and enforcers, belief becomes irrelevant. Sharia applies to everyone, Muslim or not. What matters is obedience to law, not conviction of heart – and that is what sets Islam apart from every other belief system.

Apologists may point to Sufism or personal spiritual practices within Islam. But these are the exception, not the rule. Mysticism is reserved for the few, often at odds with the legal core, and historically suppressed when it contradicts orthodoxy. The masses are not governed by mysticism – they are governed by Sharia. From the first chapter of the Quran, Al-Fatiha, Muslims are bound by ritual: it is recited 17 times a day in mandatory prayer. It denounces Christians and Jews, and affirms exclusive obedience to the Islamic path.

- Quran 1:6-7 'Guide us to the straight path, not the way of those who earned Your Anger (such as the Jews), nor of those who went astray (such as the Christians).' (Also Bukhari 782)

DAILY PRAYER SCHEDULE WITH AL-FATIHAH RECITATIONS

PRAYER	TIME OF DAY	RAK'ÂHS (SERIES)	AL-FATIHAH RECITED
Fajr	Dawn	2 rak'âhs	2 times
Dhuhr	Midday	4 rak'âhs	4 times
Asr	Afternoon	4 rak'âhs	4 times
Maghrib	Sunset	3 rak'âhs	3 times
Isha	Night	4 rak'âhs	4 times

TOTAL
17
RECITATIONS OF AL-FATIHAH PER DAY

The Word 'Religion' Is Islam's Ticket to Ride

By presenting itself as a religion instead of the deen that it is, Islam secures the legal privileges and protections reserved for spiritual belief in Western democracies. The label conceals a system of law, punishment, conquest, taxation, political loyalty, and compelled fealty to the group. It gains legitimacy through constitutional protections while using that legitimacy to undermine the very system that protects it.

In Reliance of the Traveller – a recognized manual of Islamic jurisprudence certified by al-Azhar University – spiritual obligations are eclipsed by political ones:

- Zakat finances military activities: Book h8.17 designates zakat (alms) as funding jihad.
- Calculated lying to non-Muslims is permitted and may even be obligatory if it benefits Islam (r8.2).
- Apostasy is a capital offence (o8.1–o8.4).
- Blasphemy laws silence criticism and dissent (o11.10).

In Western countries, Islam is able to exploit its classification as a religion to trigger constitutional and charter protections. Sharia tribunals have been quietly operating and, in some cases, even legalized under the banner of multiculturalism – such as under the U.K.'s Arbitration Act of 1996 or the Islamic Tribunal established in Texas in 2015. Demands for prayer rooms, halal food, hijabs, and Ramadan support in public schools and workplaces are presented either as culture or as religious rights, yet in Islamic states, refusal to observe these same rituals can result in punishment – even death.

Unlike other belief systems, Islam contains binding political, legal, military, and economic obligations. Its demands expand as its strength grows.

Doctrine Proves Governance, Not Religious Faith

Islam and Sharia are virtually synonymous in practice. Even acts commonly regarded in the West as private religious devotion are prescribed in detail: how to pray, what to recite, when to pray, how to purify oneself beforehand, and how to follow Mohammed's example.

Beyond worship, the same sources regulate contracts, speech, gender relations, dress, travel, marriage, finance, punishment, personal hygiene and public order. Islam does not merely encourage moral conduct; it demands governance.

In purely spiritual belief systems, moral rules exist as guidance, and believers choose obedience. In Islam, Sharia is not optional:

- Dress codes are legal duties.
- Dietary restrictions enforce legal penalties for violations.
- Contracts, commerce, testimony and inheritance are all regulated by Sharia.
- Criminal penalties, including hudud punishments, are legally prescribed.
- Speech is regulated; blasphemy is punishable (ROT o8.7).

Devotion is measured not simply by belief, but by conformity to a comprehensive body of prescribed conduct.

Mosques Are Strategic Assets, Not Just Places of Prayer

Islamic mosques are not merely houses of worship. From their inception, they were centers of governance, law enforcement, and military planning. Mohammad's mosque in Medina functioned as a courtroom, communications and command centre, weapons depot, diplomatic reception hall, and place of execution. It was from this mosque that raids were prepared, punishments were issued, and political rulings were declared. In Islamic doctrine, a mosque is not separated from state function – it is central to it.

Modern examples continue this tradition. In Gaza, Iraq, Syria, Iran, and Afghanistan, mosques have repeatedly been used to store weapons, conceal fighters, and launch attacks. The IDF, Syrian Army, and NATO forces have documented military operations in and around mosques being used as tactical bases. This reflects doctrinal and historical continuity. The mosque has always functioned as a strategic asset in Islam's system of governance and conquest.

- Mohammed issued military commands from the mosque pulpit, urging preparation for battle: "Strength consists in archery. Strength consists in archery. Strength consists in archery." (Muslim 1917)

Cairo Declaration: 7th Century Governance Prevails

It is therefore unsurprising that the Cairo Declaration on Human Rights in Islam (1990, revised 2020) identifies the Charter of Medina and Mohammad's final sermon as foundational sources for its conception of human rights. It then lists its articles "without prejudice to the principles of Islam." These principles are not defined in universal human terms; they are defined by reference to sacred Islamic texts, showing Sharia remains operative even when it contradicts internationally recognized human rights norms.

The Charter of Medina was Islam's first constitutional document after Mohammed's migration to Yathrib (later named Medina). It did not establish religious belief – it established political authority. It defined the Muslim ummah as "one community to the exclusion of all others," subordinated Jews and polytheists, regulated alliances and warfare, and placed Mohammad as the ultimate arbiter in all disputes among the believers. The ummah was not a confessional congregation but a political bloc. Disputes, administration, enforcement, and alliances were legal matters under Mohammed's command. (Guillaume, The Life of Muhammad, pp. 231–232)

- Quran 4:59 'O you who have believed, obey Allah and obey the Messenger and those in authority among you. And if you disagree over anything, refer it to Allah and the Messenger.'

This is governance. Mohammed is acting as head of state, judge, and war leader. Within five years, the Jewish tribes of Medina were expelled, subjugated as 'dhimmis', or killed.

The second pillar cited by the Cairo Declaration is Mohammed's 'final sermon'. In it, Muslims are commanded to "hold fast to the Book of God and the practice of His Prophet." It affirms that men may beat their wives, and that 'they are prisoners with you having no control of their persons.' This is not spiritual counsel. It is a legal command. The sermon reinforces male authority, permits physical discipline of women, and binds the community permanently to Mohammed's rulings. (Guillaume, pp. 650–652).

- Quran 4:80 "He who obeys the Messenger has obeyed Allah."
- Quran 33:21 "You have in the Messenger of Allah an excellent pattern."

Mohammed's pattern includes military conquest, political domination, expulsion of populations, and the assassination of critics and opponents. To obey him is not to adopt a private faith – it is to submit to a legal system enforced by power.

Where the Universal Declaration of Human Rights begins with the premise that all people are born free and equal, the Cairo Declaration begins with obedience. Rights exist only insofar as they do not conflict with Islamic law. Sharia is not a moral framework. It is a system of rule.

This stands in direct conflict with the Western constitutional principle that civil law is supreme and that no parallel legal authority may override constitutional rights. Islamic doctrine does not merely reject this principle; it forbids it. Sharia is the only valid legal system in Islam (Quran 5:44), and the establishment of an Islamic caliphate over all other systems is a communal obligation, "just as the judgeship is" (Reliance of the Traveller o25.2). Sharia is not subordinate within the state; it claims ultimate authority. (See also Quran 9:33, 48:28, 61:9)

- Quran 5:44 And whoever does not judge by what Allah has revealed – then it is they who are the disbelievers.
- Quran 33:36 It is not for a believing man or woman, when Allah and His Messenger have decided a matter, to have any other choice in their affair."

The Enforcers of Doctrine Are Not Pastors – They Are Jurists

Imams, mullahs, and sheikhs are perceived in the West as spiritual guides. In Islamic doctrine, they are legal authorities. Their role is to interpret and enforce Sharia – not to offer pastoral care or counsel. As in Iran, they sit at the apex of legal, political, and punitive power. Whether issuing fatwas, validating punishments, or instructing armed men from the pulpit, they function not as religious leaders, but as enforcers of a divine legal code. It is through their rulings that dissent is crushed, apostates condemned, and entire populations brought under control.

What Happens When Islam Wins?

Islam does not prepare the soul for the afterlife. It prepares the world for submission. It elevates the jihadi, suppresses the critical thinker, and replaces the human need for spiritual connection with ritual prayer, loyalty to Mohammed, and the enforcement of Sharia – the system through which Allah's will is imposed on earth.

It punishes the conscience and rewards the enforcer. Where Islam gains power, the result is not spiritual renewal – but legal domination. Apostates are killed. Critics are silenced. Women are controlled. Minorities are taxed or erased. The vulnerable suffer most.

The consequences are already visible throughout Western institutions.

2. Sharia in Western Institutions

The 1979 Turning Point: Sharia as Global Educational Policy

The institutional campaigns now promoted under banners such as "Islamophobia" did not emerge spontaneously within Western democracies. Their ideological roots lie in Mecca.

In November 1979, armed militants seized the Grand Mosque, occupied the Kaaba, and declared that Islam had strayed from its true path. Their demand was not political reform but the restoration of foundational Islam under Sharia. Faced with an unprecedented crisis, the Saudi monarchy secured a fatwa authorising military intervention (Trofimov). The price was a renewed commitment to fund the global expansion of Islam through dawa with oil revenues. Other wealthy Gulf states, particularly Qatar, would later pursue similar strategies.

That decision marked a turning point. Dawa was transformed from a largely regional activity into a coordinated international enterprise. Vast financial resources were directed toward mosques, universities, charities, educational programmes, publishing, media, and advocacy organizations throughout the non-Muslim world. The objective was not merely the promotion of Islamic belief but the expansion of a deen whose own sources describe Sharia as the ordained path for all of mankind.

Education became one of the principal vehicles through which this strategy advanced. As described in A Civilizational Reckoning, Islamic educational materials increasingly appeared in schools, universities, teacher-training programmes, and public institutions throughout the West (Davidson; ISGAP; Ellinger 2025). Rather than encouraging objective examination of Islamic doctrine, they present a carefully curated version of

Islam while discouraging critical scrutiny of its legal and political dimensions.

The institutional campaigns now surrounding "Islamophobia" have developed within the international dawa infrastructure that expanded after 1979. Governments, universities, and NGOs that now mark these events operate within that broader environment, whether or not they recognize its origins. What began as a violent demand for the return to foundational Islam has, over almost five decades, transformed into policy, funding, and legislation across the non-Muslim world. Campaigns that appear to encourage tolerance or inclusion operate alongside long-established efforts to normalise Islamic legal and political concepts within non-Muslim societies.

When Accommodation Becomes Institutional Capture

One mechanism by which this occurs is the informational guides produced by Muslim employee networks in Western countries. These guides go far beyond normal religious privilege. They introduce Islamic rules, expectations, and sensitivities into the structure of public workplaces, including recommendations intended to reshape institutions to comply with Sharia-derived norms.

A multitude of such guides are published annually throughout the West, urging Muslims to become activists in a wide range of professional and public settings. They explain how to assert Sharia requirements in schools, universities, workplaces, hospitals, law enforcement, transportation, and the media, while simultaneously instructing those institutions on how to facilitate Islamic norms.

One such guide, produced by Canada's Muslim Federal Employees Network, instructs managers to allow up to three daily prayers during work hours, provide image-free private rooms marking the qibla (direction of prayer), and to avoid handshakes or private meetings with opposite-sex employees. It tells managers to avoid alcohol-centred events, modify schedules throughout Ramadan – a moving lunar observance that shifts each year – and ensure employees receive additional leave during its final ten days. This reverses the usual expectation that employees adapt to the workplace, in favour of the workplace adapting to Islam.

This represents a clear instance of creedism: the institutional privileging of an Islamic deen inside public bodies that are meant to remain neutral. More strikingly, the guide directs employees to seek "religious literacy" only from Muslims and Muslim organizations. It promotes anti-Islamophobia training delivered by the same groups and encourages Muslim employees to use it to make workplace demands. This is not an employee network operating for the benefit of all staff. It is an effort to institutionalize a single deen-based worldview – and not necessarily one that every Muslim may wish to comply with.

Similar patterns have appeared in other Western countries, where employee networks and advocacy groups push for comparable concessions in public institutions. While the details vary, the underlying mechanism is the same: the gradual embedding of Sharia norms into organizations that are constitutionally required to remain neutral.

Sharia, however, is enforced socially as well as individually. The pressure to conform does not come only from institutions but from within the Muslim collective itself. This dynamic is explicit in Islamic sources. Mohammed said,

- "And I command you with five that Allah commanded me: Listening and obeying, Jihad, Hijrah [migration], and the Jama'ah." (Tirmidhi 2863)

Reliance of the Traveller q0.2 describes the duty of enjoining right and forbidding wrong as "the most important fundamental of the religion" and outlines escalating levels of enforcement, up to the use of force when necessary.

Jama'ah requires outward conformity, collective alignment, and obedience to the group. Where Muslims live as minorities, this obligation does not disappear. It is managed. As the minority expands and gains strength, so too does the pressure exerted on Muslims who do not conform.

What Management is NOT told

Guides produced by Muslim employee networks do more than request accommodation. They advance a deeper and deceptive shift.

When Muslims are unable to fully apply Sharia, Islamic jurisprudence permits temporary concessions under darura – necessity overriding prohibition – until conditions make fuller implementation possible. Managers are not told this. Instead, the guide produced by Canada's Muslim Federal Employees Network does the opposite: rather than permitting individual adaptation under non-Islamic authority, it seeks full compliance with Sharia norms by the institution itself.

In doing so, the guide advances Sharia and the Islamization of the country by removing the very conditions under which darura operates. The freedom to choose non-halal finance, schools, food, and clothing in a non-Islamic state is gradually eroded, not by coercion, but by institutional realignment that eliminates the option.

The workplace is treated as the entity that must bend.

Where full adherence to Sharia is not possible, devout Muslims are expected either to work toward conditions in which Islamic law can be fully observed – that is, the expansion of dar al-Islam – or to relocate, as indicated in Quran 4:97:

- "Indeed, those whom the angels take [in death] while wronging themselves... The angels will say, 'Was not the earth of Allah spacious [enough] for you to emigrate therein?'"

Failing to mention the principle of darura to management cannot be considered an oversight. Islamic jurisprudence permits concealment and strategic disclosure in pursuit of Sharia objectives, particularly where Muslims operate under non-Islamic authority. The result is a one-way presentation of obligations: institutions are told what they must provide, while the doctrinal flexibility already available to Muslim employees is strategically withheld.

- "Scholars say that there is no harm in giving a misleading impression if required by an interest countenanced by Sacred Law [Sharia]..." (ROT r10.3)
- "It is permissible to lie when the goal is permissible... obligatory if the goal is obligatory." "But it is religiously more precautionary in all such cases to employ words that give a misleading impression..." (ROT r8.2)

Mohammed himself applied the principle of darura. Aisha reported that when he missed the night prayer due to pain or any other reason, he observed twelve rak'ahs during the daytime (Muslim 746e). The Quran likewise states "There is no sin upon him" when permitted options are unavailable (Quran 2:173, 6:145, 16:115).

How Conformity Is Enforced

Pressure, often invisible to outsiders, is exerted by more observant Muslims on those who would otherwise keep their beliefs private. This is well documented on university campuses, where Muslim students who prefer quiet observance are increasingly pushed to conform to Islamic norms of dress, behaviour, and political activism – to conform to the Jama'ah (Husain 2021). What is presented externally as "religious sensitivity" functions internally as enforcement.

- Mohammed said: "He who amongst you sees something abominable [not Sharia] should modify it with the help of his hand; and if he has not strength enough to do it, then he should do it with his tongue, and if he has not strength enough to do it, then he should (abhor it) from his heart, and that is the least of faith." (Muslim 49a)

It is therefore not the most assimilated or private Muslims who drive jihad or Sharia-compliant restructuring of institutions. It is those most committed to ideological conformity, discipline, and collective obligation. The same people who insist on public observance, gender segregation, and behavioural rules are those who view resistance, enforcement, and expansion as Islamic duties rather than personal choices.

This distinction is routinely ignored in public discourse. Violence and coercion are treated as deviations, while conformity is framed as harmless piety. In reality, they sit on the same doctrinal continuum.

The Recommendation Itself Is the Red Flag

In any secular democracy, public employees should not be compelled or even requested to follow Sharia-derived behavioural rules, nor should public institutions be adapted to the ritual architecture of Islam. A government that facilitates or implements the recommendations of a creed-based ideology as though they were normative is not neutral. It is creedist.

The principle becomes clear when one considers the practical consequences. If every community demanded what this guide requires for Muslims, the public sector would quickly become unworkable. One can easily imagine Catholics requesting scheduled pauses for the Angelus, private confession time, and chapels in every building; Jews requesting halachic-compliant kitchens, Sabbath-adjusted hours and gendered meeting rules; Sikhs requesting kirpan-adapted security procedures and ritual-purification space; or Indigenous groups requesting ceremony rooms, smudging protocols and elder-supervised decision making. The system cannot function when each belief system, deen or cultural group inserts its own legal or ritual code into public administration regardless of how those demands are framed.

This problem is not limited to the guides themselves. The committees and networks that produce them are also creedist in nature. They function as agents of creedism, working to embed Sharia rules and expectations into public institutions under the guise of inclusion. The result is that public institutions increasingly adopt behavioural expectations derived not from constitutional principles but from creed-based doctrine.

Canada provides a clear example, but similar patterns are unfolding throughout the West.

"Islamophobia" as a Tool of Sharia

Western democracies have increasingly adopted measures that shield Islamic doctrine from criticism under the banner of combating "Islamophobia." The term itself, along with related charges of racism and religious discrimination, confuses a body of doctrine with a race or a private belief and thereby attempts to place sharia beyond ordinary scrutiny. In 2017, the Canadian Parliament adopted Motion M-103, a non-binding resolution calling on the government to condemn "Islamophobia" and to study ways of addressing systemic racism and religious discrimination. Although it created no new law, the motion marked an important political shift by elevating "Islamophobia" as a distinct public policy concern. In 2021, the federal government established January 29 as the National Day of Remembrance of the Québec City Mosque Attack and Action against Islamophobia.

Both of these events were promoted by NCCM – originally CAIR-Canada, the Canadian arm of a U.S.-based lobby group with a history of foreign funding – now rebranded and in receipt of taxpayer-funded grants. It is also authorised by the Canadian Council of Imams to collect zakat 'in the cause of Allah' (fi sabilillah), the doctrinal category that finances the many forms of jihad.

Its parent organization in the United States was an unindicted co-conspirator in the Holy Land Foundation terror-financing trial and has since been designated by Texas as a terrorist-linked entity. Yet in Canada it is granted political access, media promotion, educational and institutional authority. As Canada's 'Special Representative on Combatting Islamophobia,' NCCM's former Director of Communications, Ms Elghawaby, argued that the absence of Muslim prayer facilities in federal workplaces constituted workplace "Islamophobia."

In notes disclosed under Access to Information, her office characterized the lack of provision for Muslim prayer during business hours as "Islamophobia in the workplace." She subsequently pressed federal managers to install Muslim prayer rooms within federal offices, even lodging complaints when the response from the Canada Revenue Agency was not sufficiently prompt.

Each January 29, this convergence of government policy and Islamic advocacy is publicly reinforced. Monuments are lit green in honour of Mohammed – his favourite colour – schools hold lectures, labour unions and public departments signal their solidarity.

NCCM supplies teachers with educational materials that move well beyond remembrance. Students are encouraged to wear symbols of solidarity, produce public declarations explaining their support, create videos, share their reflections online, and become "allies" in a coordinated campaign. Films, classroom discussions, and prescribed activities all reinforce the same approved narrative while omitting any examination of Islamic doctrine or the difference between criticism of ideas and hostility toward individuals. Rather than encouraging independent inquiry, they are encouraging children to be creedist. The programme conditions students to associate questioning Islam with prejudice, replacing critical thinking with emotional identification and social conformity.

Much more than a memorial for victims, it is a political event created to advance the institutional protection of a system of law that silences criticism and punishes dissent. That system is called Sharia.

Canada has effectively institutionalised the concept of "Islamophobia," creating an environment in which 40 million people risk being reported, investigated, or professionally sanctioned for voicing concern about a deen that explicitly seeks global supremacy. The Islamophobia-Motivated Incident Reporting Tool (IMIRT) is actively promoted to help track and report 'hate-motivated' incidents.

What Is Really Being Protected?

On March 15 – the United Nations' "International Day to Combat Islamophobia," established following an OIC-sponsored resolution – the pattern is repeated across multiple Western countries. Every year, citizens throughout Western democracies are invited to participate in a carefully coordinated public narrative: that Muslims are uniquely vulnerable and that criticism of Islam increasingly falls within the boundaries of "Islamophobia."

This is a dawa campaign to embed into Western law and culture the belief that the Islamic deen may not be questioned, examined, or opposed. It is a clear expression of creedism at the level of the state: the institutional decision to grant Islam special consideration while every other belief system remains open to debate.

These events increasingly serve as cover for a supremacist doctrine that demands political and legal immunity – a doctrine that divides the world between those who submit to its rule and those who do not. The Quran, hadith, and legal rulings of Sharia establish this division without ambiguity:

Supremacy: "It is He who has sent His Messenger with guidance and the deen of truth to prevail over all deen." (Quran 9:33)

Conquest: "Fight them until there is no more fitnah and the religion is all for Allah." (Quran 8:39)

Silence dissent: "Among the things that constitute apostasy: ... denials of Allah's existence, eternity, or permanence, as well as denials of the universally agreed-upon attributes. Showing contempt for Allah's name, command, prohibition, promise, or threat; denying a verse of the Quran whose authenticity is unanimously agreed upon." (Reliance of the Traveller o8.7(4))

Apostasy: "Whoever changes his Islamic religion, then kill him." (Bukhari 6922)

Yet Islam receives special consideration, while those who question its doctrines increasingly face investigation, professional sanction, or public condemnation. The label "Islamophobia" has become one of the principal mechanisms through which this inversion is achieved.

Institutional Accommodation

The widespread misclassification of Islam as a religion rather than a comprehensive deen has profound institutional consequences. Western governments, universities, charities, labour organizations, NGOs, and public bodies routinely treat Islamic organizations as ordinary religious partners without examining their doctrinal objectives or the foreign funding that supports them.

Special privileges facilitating Sharia observance have been incorporated across a wide spectrum. Institutions once trusted as neutral – school boards, hospitals, museums, courtrooms, and even law enforcement – no longer are. Schools and universities in particular shape future citizens, making them uniquely valuable to any movement seeking long-term societal influence. The extensive use of educational materials that omit, minimise, or reinterpret foundational Islamic doctrine has contributed to a widespread misunderstanding of Islam among both students in secular schools and those in Islamic schools. The results of that education are visible in the workforce, where many of those former students now serve as politicians, policy advisors, lawyers, journalists, and institutional decision-makers.

A similar pattern has emerged in immigration, the growth of parallel communities, and public administration (Kassam). Accommodation is generally assumed to be an unqualified social good, while little attention is given to the legal or ideological expectations that may accompany it. Discussion of doctrine is replaced by discussions of diversity, inclusion, or cultural sensitivity.

Western states once routinely recorded religious affiliation in census and administrative data. That practice has largely been abandoned. Nationality is now treated as the relevant category, even though citizenship can be acquired, populations are mixed, and the same passport can mask sharply different doctrinal commitments. Afghanistan, once a centre of Buddhist civilization, is now a major source of committed jihad; the land did not change, the doctrine did. When a creed is structurally hostile to those outside it – ranking its own members as "the best of creatures" and those who reject it as "the worst of creatures" – the refusal to collect or publish data by belief removes the most informative variable from public view. Islam is a doctrine of supremacy, submission, and separation but it is not a race, neither is it a nationality (Quran 98:6-7).

The Mechanics of Institutional Denial

The continued expansion of Sharia-derived norms within Western institutions rarely occurs through explicit endorsement of Islamic law. More commonly, it proceeds through institutional reluctance to examine the doctrine at all. Islamic legal concepts are reframed as matters of culture, identity, or religious freedom rather than law, while discussion of jihad, apostasy, supremacy, and Sharia is replaced by appeals to tolerance, equity, or social cohesion. Citizens who examine Islamic primary sources increasingly become the focus of censure, while organizations advancing Islamic objectives are treated as representatives of an ordinary faith community.

The result is a form of plausible deniability. Institutions need not defend Sharia directly if they first discourage examination of what Sharia teaches. Public attention shifts from doctrine to the motives of those who discuss it, allowing difficult questions about Islamic law and authority to remain unaddressed.

Western institutions have increasingly fostered a culture in which defending existing laws, customs, or constitutional principles is treated with suspicion, while deference is assumed to be the moral default. Objection is readily reclassified as intolerance or bigotry.

The Inversion of Justice: Creedism in the Courtroom

If a weak and ill-informed majority faces a strong, united, and preferentially treated minority, the balance of power shifts rapidly. This is visible not only in policy but in courtrooms. A British mother who posted (then quickly deleted) a regrettable tweet after the Southport child murders received a 31-month prison sentence, while a Muslim man who attacked a Quran burner with a knife received no jail time at all. The initial attempt to hush up the Southport murders – and the heavy-handed response to public anger when the truth emerged – only accelerated the conflict. In Germany, a 20-year-old woman was sentenced to a weekend in jail for online comments about nine migrant men who gang-raped a 15-year-old girl; yet eight of the perpetrators received no jail time despite DNA evidence.

This inversion has nothing to do with race. It has everything to do with Creedism. Sharia classifies non-Muslims as subordinate. It regulates public life, education, speech, gender relations, and belief itself. When institutions refuse to acknowledge this, they do not preserve harmony. Quite the opposite.

When Sharia Becomes State Law

Those who argue that Sharia is merely a personal moral code or spiritual guide need only examine countries where it forms the basis of state authority. Once Sharia becomes the recognized law of the land, it no longer governs only those who choose to follow it. It governs everyone.

Iran provides one of the clearest contemporary examples.

Following the 1979 Islamic Revolution, Iran formally established an Islamic state in which political authority derives from Islamic authority. It is not a state with Islam; it is an Islamic deen with a state. In Western constitutional systems, the offices of head of state, commander-in-chief, chief justice, and senior religious leader are separate. Under Iran's Islamic constitution, those functions ultimately converge in the office of the Supreme Leader.

Accordingly, the Supreme Leader is not merely a Western-style "religious leader" but the country's highest legal, political, and military authority – as was Mohammed. The result is the institutional enforcement of Islamic law throughout public life.

This is what Sharia looks like when exercised through the powers of the state:

- Compulsory hijab for all women from the age of nine lunar years (or earlier), enforced by state law, surveillance, fines, arrests, and other penalties (Quran 24:31; 33:59)
- Gender segregation in schools, public institutions, sporting events, and other aspects of public life.
- Morality police empowered to arrest and punish citizens for noncompliance according to official interpretations of Islamic standards.
- Apostasy and blasphemy laws, punishable by death (Reliance of the Traveller o8.1)

- Censorship, with books, films, music, journalism, and online expression subject to Islamic review.
- Islamic courts applying Sharia-based legal principles and hudud punishments including amputation.
- Non-Muslims barred from the presidency and the highest offices of state
- Academic, professional, and public life subject to ideological conformity, with criticism of Islamic law or core religious doctrine carrying serious risks to employment, advancement, professional licensing, surveillance, prosecution, or imprisonment.
- State surveillance of private life, with citizens reporting on one another for un-Islamic conduct
- Restrictions on non-Muslim communities, affecting employment, education, religious practice, and legal equality.
- Intrusion into private life, including regulation of personal appearance, relationships, and behaviour through state institutions and surveillance.

Iran is a multi-ethnic society comprising Muslims and non-Muslims alike. Yet Sharia applies irrespective of ethnicity or personal belief. There is no meaningful opt-out provision for those who reject Islam.

The End Point of Accommodation

The Muslim employee guides, publicly funded advocacy organizations, "Islamophobia" campaigns, curriculum revisions, and institutional partnerships discussed throughout this chapter are not disconnected developments. They are early-stage expressions of the same sharia-based order that, once it gains state power, produces the kind of society now visible in Iran.

When the Islamic deen is treated as merely a private religion, Western institutions extend it legal and cultural protections that they would not grant to any other comprehensive political and legal system. Deference becomes the default. Critique is reframed as prejudice. Over time, the distinction between private belief and public authority is steadily eroded.

Iran demonstrates what happens when that process reaches its logical conclusion. The same sources that prescribe compulsory hijab, gender segregation, apostasy laws, hudud punishments, and the subordination of non-Muslims are not confined to one country. They remain authoritative in Islamic jurisprudence regardless of geography. What changes is only the degree of power available to enforce them.

3. The Human Cost

Can a Civilization Evolve Beyond Its Founding Precedent?

Every civilization has committed acts that later generations regard with horror. Medieval Europe employed torture. Henry VIII executed political opponents and religious dissenters. Vlad III of Wallachia became infamous for impaling thousands of his enemies. Ironically, Vlad himself spent part of his youth as a hostage at the Ottoman court, where he witnessed and is widely believed to have learned the very methods for which he was later known. These events form part of history, but they do not define the legal or moral obligations of those civilizations today.

Western civilization gradually separated historical practice from enduring principle.

No Anglican is expected to torture prisoners because Henry VIII once did. Their actions are studied as history, not preserved as binding precedent. No European legal system derives authority from Vlad the Impaler. Neither were those political monarchs ever construed as religious figures. They may explain the past, but they do not rule the present. Law evolved. Moral understanding evolved. Political institutions evolved. The actions of rulers became subject to criticism, revision, and sometimes rejection.

The Islamic deen presents a fundamentally different model.

Mohammed is not regarded simply as the founder of Islam or its first political leader. He is presented by the Quran as the perfect example for believers to follow for all time. His judgments, conduct, approvals, and practices form a primary source of Islamic law. His life is therefore not merely history; it establishes precedent. Sharia developed by asking not what later generations thought appropriate, but what Allah revealed and how Mohammed applied those revelations.

Precedent Endures

The issue is not whether individual Muslims today choose to imitate every action recorded in the classical sources. Many do not. Others do. The issue is that the sources themselves remain authoritative and available to those who choose to apply them. Where Western civilizations treat the actions of historical rulers as products of their time, Islam treats the conduct of Mohammed as normative because it is understood to reflect divine guidance.

This helps explain why debates surrounding Islam so often differ from debates surrounding other civilizations. When historians criticize Henry VIII or the Inquisition, they are criticizing historical institutions whose authority has long since disappeared. When one examines Mohammed's conduct or the legal rulings derived from it, one is examining sources that continue to occupy a central place in Islamic jurisprudence today.

That difference has practical consequences.

Western societies generally assume that all civilizations evolve in the same manner – that objectionable practices naturally become historical curiosities as moral understanding advances. Yet a system whose highest legal authorities are regarded as divinely revealed and binding operates according to a different principle. The question is no longer whether a historical practice should continue, but whether divine precedent can be set aside.

For Islam, it cannot.

One of the clearest consequences of misclassifying Islam as just another religion is that Western societies continue to tolerate practices carried out in its name that they would condemn in any other context. Female genital mutilation (FGM) is one such example.

The Price of Creedism

In 2018, a United States federal judge ruled that the federal law prohibiting female genital mutilation exceeded Congress's constitutional authority, leading prosecutors to abandon their appeal. While individual states remain free to legislate against the practice, the decision represented a significant setback in efforts to eradicate a procedure internationally recognized as a serious violation of the rights of women and girls.

The timing could scarcely have been worse. UNICEF reports that progress toward eliminating female genital mutilation continues to lag behind population growth, meaning that despite decades of international campaigning, the total number of girls at risk continues to increase.

Although female genital mutilation is also practised within some non-Muslim communities, its prevalence is markedly higher in populations where it is associated with Islamic tradition. One recent estimate found that approximately 23.5 percent of Muslim women had undergone some form of female genital mutilation, compared with fewer than two percent of non-Muslim women (Flynn). As migration has increased, so too has the presence of the practice within Western countries. Supporters appeal to custom or religious obligation, citing Islamic tradition and narrations encouraging adherence to Allah's created order.

- "So direct your face toward the deen, inclining to truth. The fitrah of Allah upon which He created mankind... That is the upright deen." (Quran 30:30)

Hadith then describe the fitra (natural disposition) as personal hygiene including circumcision, trimming the moustache, clipping the nails, plucking the underarm hair, and other practices.

- Dawud 5271: A woman used to perform circumcision in Medina. Mohammed said to her: "Do not cut severely as that is better for a woman and more desirable for a husband."

- Ibn Majah 608 (Aisha): "When the two circumcised parts meet, then bath is obligatory. The Messenger of Allah and I did that, and we bathed."

The medical consequences are neither uncertain nor minor. Decades of peer-reviewed research, including studies published by the World Health Organization consistently demonstrate that female genital mutilation produces lifelong physical, sexual, reproductive, and psychological harm. The procedure is commonly performed without anaesthesia, exposing young girls to severe pain, haemorrhage, shock, infection, urinary retention, and extensive tissue damage. In some cases, death results from blood loss or sepsis.

Those who survive frequently endure lifelong complications. Chronic pelvic pain, recurrent urinary tract infections, menstrual disorders, infertility resulting from infection and scar tissue, painful scarring, and urinary dysfunction are widely documented. Pregnancy presents additional risks. Women who have undergone female genital mutilation experience higher rates of prolonged labour, postpartum haemorrhage, caesarean delivery, obstetric tearing, and neonatal mortality. The World Health Organization's most recent review reports substantially increased rates of postpartum haemorrhage, higher caesarean section rates, and an elevated risk of death among newborn infants.

These outcomes are well known. They have been documented repeatedly by medical researchers, international health organizations, and human rights bodies. The continuing prevalence of female genital mutilation therefore cannot be explained by ignorance of its consequences.

The same pattern appears across a range of other practices.

Once Sharia holds sway, forced marriage, repeated cousin marriage with its associated increase in inherited genetic disorders, honour killings, compulsory veiling, unequal legal status for women, and mob violence become commonplace (Nushuz). Corporal punishments such as beheading, stoning, and amputation are likewise prescribed.

Sharia also exempts parents and grandparents from legal accountability when they kill their own children. While the Quran recounts the killing of a boy whose future disobedience was feared (Quran 18:80-81), Reliance of the Traveller states: "There is no expiation for killing one's own child or grandchild" (o1.2(4)).

Reluctance to confront such practices has consequences beyond the treatment of Muslim women and girls. It also leads Western societies to downplay or ignore the deen's provisions regarding non-Muslims.

Slavery remains explicitly permitted under Sharia, provided the enslaved person is not originally Muslim. Quran 4:24 includes among the lawful "those whom your right hands possess." Most Muslim-majority states have abolished slavery by civil statute, yet classical law still permits it, and constitutions that subordinate legislation to Sharia leave the door open. Public discussion of slavery still centres on the Atlantic trade of the sixteenth to nineteenth centuries, while this longer history receives little attention. Yet when political conditions allow, the practice reveals itself with doctrinal cover. Recent testimony at a United Nations event in Geneva, from Druze victims in Syria and Yazidi survivors, described abduction, forced conversion, rape, torture and execution. Iraqi jihadists enslaved some 6,000 Yazidi women and girls. Prosecutions in the region have generally proceeded under terrorism law rather than for the enslavement itself. These are not isolated excesses. They follow the classification of such communities as permissible targets for enslavement and sexual use.

Islamic doctrine is clear on this point. Unbelievers are described as unclean, and only veiled women are considered respectable. Ibn Kathir's commentary on Quran 33:59 records the ruling: "Ibn Abbas said that Allah commanded the believing women, when they went out of their houses for some need, to cover their faces from above their heads with the jilbab, leaving only one eye showing.... If they do that, it will be known that they are free, and that they are not servants or whores." Failure to veil can therefore be used within the tradition to shift responsibility for abuse onto the woman herself. This is the ordained way of Islam, linking obedience to Allah with the finality of Mohammed's example.

- Quran 33:36 "it is not for a believing man or a believing woman to have any choice in a matter once Allah and His Messenger have decided it."

Violence Against Civilians

The same pattern of classification and permitted violence identified above was visible in the 2025 attack at Bondi Beach in Australia. Two Muslim men opened fire from an elevated footbridge on mostly Jewish families celebrating Hanukkah below. The victims were unarmed and had no means of sheltering or escape. The attack was not an aberration from Islamic doctrine. It followed directly from it.

Islamic texts repeatedly place non-Muslims in a category beneath full moral consideration:

- Quran 7:179 states they "are like livestock. Rather, they are more astray."
- Quran 8:55 calls them "the worst of creatures in the sight of Allah."
- Quran 7:176 compares the one who rejects guidance to "a dog: if you drive him away, he lolls his tongue out, or if you leave him alone, he still lolls his tongue out."
- Quran 62:5 likens them to "a donkey carrying books without understanding."

Mohammed himself associated a group of Israelites with rats (Bukhari 3305). When a population is placed in the category of vermin, the logic of extermination follows. Once people are no longer viewed as fully human, ordinary moral restraints no longer apply.

This mindset produces patterns visible in multiple contexts: fathers and sons hunting Jews together, groups of men participating in organized rape of non-Muslim girls, and communities that shelter perpetrators rather than reporting them. There is no shame attached because the victims have already been removed from the circle of moral concern. Instead of a bounty, participants are promised booty, honour, and paradise:

- Mohammed said that none of the people of Paradise would wish to return to the world except the martyr, who would love to be killed ten times in Allah's cause because of the honour he has seen (Tirmidhi 1661).

The doctrine also provides mechanisms for silence and concealment:

- Reliance of the Traveller r8.2 permits lying when concealing a Muslim from an oppressor.
- Reliance of the Traveller w52.1 instructs believers never to show others the weak points of the Muslims.
- Tirmidhi 1930 states that whoever covers the faults of a Muslim, Allah will cover his faults for him in the world and the Hereafter.

Mohammed himself established the precedent. After the migration to Medina he personally led or authorised dozens of military expeditions. During the sacking of Khaybar in 628, the Jews emerged carrying their farming tools and were told their settlement was destroyed (Bukhari 4200).

- "The Prophet (peace be upon him) prayed the morning prayer near Khaybar while it was still dark. Then he said: "Allahu akbar. Khaybar is ruined. When we descend upon the open ground of a people, how evil is the morning of those who were warned."

  They came out running in the streets. The Prophet killed the fighting men and took the children and women captive. Among the captives was Safiyya. She first went to Dihya al-Kalbi, then she went to the Prophet, and he made her manumission her dowry.

- The Messenger of Allah took out his fifth from the booty of Khaybar, and divided the rest of it among those who attended the battle and among those who were away from it but attend the expedition of al-Hudaybiyyah.

Many were killed, others enslaved, and the remainder reduced to paying jizya. Quran 8:67 states that it is not for a prophet to have captives until he has made a great slaughter in the land.

And true to that directive this is precisely what happened at the Nova music festival on 7 October 2023, when 364 attendees and 15 police officers were killed, while 44 festival-goers were taken hostage. Across Israel that day, more than 1,200 people were killed and approximately 251 were abducted and taken into Gaza.

Emotional attachment to non-Muslims would make the required acts of separation and hostility impossible. The doctrine resolves the tension by repeatedly forbidding such attachment except as a precaution (Quran 3:28).

Ibn Kathir's commentary on this verse makes the underlying attitude explicit: "We smile in the face of some people although our hearts curse them." "The Tuqyah [deception] is allowed until the Day of Resurrection." Allah said (Bukhari)

Islamic theology further removes personal guilt from acts of violence by transferring agency to Allah:

- Quran 8:17 states: "You did not kill them, but Allah killed them. And you did not throw when you threw, but Allah threw."

When responsibility is displaced onto the divine, remorse becomes unnecessary. Celebration becomes intelligible.

After the Bondi Beach attack, one observer described it as "dishonourable." The reaction revealed more about the observer than the attack. To describe an act as dishonourable assumes a shared understanding of honour. An Islamic deen does not share the Western conception. Words such as righteous, just, and truthful refer to obedience to Islam and Sharia, not to universal ethical principles. Quran 49:13 states that the most noble in the sight of Allah is the most righteous of you – that is, the one who most faithfully conforms to Islamic norms.

This explains why family members sometimes participate in attacks, why communities shelter perpetrators, and why jihadists can phone parents to boast of their kills and expect praise. The same logic that once allowed people to speak of shooting rabbits without moral discomfort also allows the killing of non-Muslims to be treated as an act worthy of honour.

Age, innocence, intelligence, or circumstance do not change the classification. This is why non-Muslims consistently misread Islamic violence. They do not grasp the low status the doctrine assigns to them, nor the high honour it accords to jihad. They continue to interpret Islamic moral language through a Western lens, and are therefore repeatedly shocked by acts that are fully consistent with the texts and precedents of the deen.

The same failure appears in Western courts. When the perpetrator's actions follow the doctrine, the response is often to diagnose mental illness rather than to examine the teachings that render those actions coherent and, within the deen, honourable. The doctrine itself continues to be granted the status of a religion.

This divergence also appears at the international level. While most nations accept the Universal Declaration of Human Rights, the Organization of Islamic Cooperation issued its own Cairo Declaration on Human Rights in Islam precisely because the UDHR was deemed incompatible with Sharia. All rights in that declaration are explicitly subject to Islamic law. Member states of the OIC nevertheless sit as full voting members of the United Nations, present resolutions, and chair committees while adhering to a standard of human rights antithetical to the UDHR. No other belief system requires such a parallel instrument.

The past two decades alone have seen thousands killed in jihadist attacks across Western and non-Western cities. Europol continues to warn of the persistent threat. In 2025, Christmas markets in Germany were heavily fortified or cancelled altogether for fear of attack. Yet, former military sites and public buildings are being repurposed to house large numbers of adult male asylum seekers from Islamic countries, with little to no transparency regarding their identities, backgrounds, or ideological commitments.

As long as the doctrine of Islam is treated as beyond criticism, the number who suffer under its authority will continue to expand.

4. Following False Guides: The Trojan Horse

Brave voices defending the foundations of liberal democracy are being marginalised, while political, media, and institutional elites continue to follow seductive but false guides who promise that Islam can be managed or moderated. This retreat is not accidental. It is the result of denial, misclassification, and a lack of political will.

Western societies now face a clear choice. One path requires honest engagement with the doctrine, clear legal barriers against parallel systems, and firm protection of universal human rights. The other continues the current pattern of denial, incremental concession, and civilizational retreat.

A major reason the second path remains so tempting is the persistent presence of what can only be described as a modern Trojan Horse. It looks friendly. It speaks the language of peace and integration. It poses for photographs with politicians and assures the public it is different from the extremists. Yet it comes from the same doctrinal blueprint and carries the same cargo.

In 2009, Sam Solomon and E. Al Maqdisi wrote a short book about this dynamic. They called it The Modern Day Trojan Horse: The Islamic Doctrine of Immigration, Accepting Freedom or Imposing Islam.

The real issue is not the horse itself, but the source that keeps producing these horses, generation after generation. The horse is driven by self-preservation. It wants to protect itself and ensure future generations of horses. So it never identifies who builds the horses. It cannot name them without confronting its origins in the Quran and the life of Mohammed. Instead, it lives in denial, insisting it can help defeat the dangerous cargo while refusing to acknowledge why the cargo exists in the first place.

This brings us to the contemporary, polished Trojan Horse; it presents itself as the solution while remaining inseparable from the doctrine that produces the problem.

Western societies, having misclassified Islam as a religion rather than a deen, have created the conditions in which these horses flourish. A population that no longer clearly understands what it is dealing with becomes easy prey for guides who promise solutions while protecting the doctrinal source from examination.

A perfect example is Mohammad Tawhidi, now presented as an "Imam of Peace" despite having no recognised credentials according to multiple reliable sources. The Al Mustafa seminary in Qom stated he withdrew in 2012 and is not competent to lecture, and the Australian National Imams Council does not recognise him.

He is a senior figure in the Global Imams Council (GIC), which presents itself as the first transnational body of Muslim faith leaders. It claims over 1,500 scholars and 800 communities worldwide – a tiny fraction of the estimated 400,000 to one million imams globally. Its branding and language are carefully designed to make non-Muslim politicians feel they are hearing from mainstream Islam. The official message is consistent: the problem is the Muslim Brotherhood, extremists and radicals – not the doctrine itself. By shifting the focus onto people and organizations, the GIC diverts attention from the texts and legal rulings that remain binding on every adherent. The Brotherhood is portrayed as a deviation, while the GIC positions itself as the moderate alternative – even though it too is rejected by mainstream Islamic authorities and represents only a minute proportion of the global scholarly community.

Nevertheless, Western politicians and media have treated Tawhidi as a representative voice. Once again, Western authorities turn to insiders who adhere to the doctrine to explain how to manage it – nominal Muslims claiming to oppose extremism while still adhering to a belief system whose primary texts are the source of the problem.

I watched Tawhidi in a recorded session with Canadian parliamentarians who were visibly delighted to hear his message and his promise of a seventeen-volume "encyclopedia" on the Muslim Brotherhood with a special volume dedicated to Canada. There was money, media attention, and the comforting illusion that a Muslim was finally going to solve the problem they themselves created through reckless immigration policy and complete ignorance of Sharia. His performance was pure theatre: the costume, the cadence, the hand movements. Showmanship at its finest.

- "Had only ten Jews (amongst their chiefs) believe me, all the Jews would definitely have believed me." (Bukhari 3941)

At this event Tawhidi declared that the Muslim Brotherhood does not speak for Islam. But neither does his group. In reality, nobody speaks for Islam except Allah and Mohammed. The doctrine is fixed. It is not up for revision. It is not moderated, diluted, or edited by any council, conference, or self-appointed spokesman. Offering seventeen volumes on an organisation he insists does not speak for Islam only highlights the diversion. Western politicians, enchanted by the performance, fail to notice they are being steered away from the doctrine itself.

Who is the real audience? Some Muslims, perhaps, but primarily non-Muslims desperate to be reassured that Islam has a moderate centre that simply needs support and exposure.

The deen's real influence rests elsewhere. Canada's "Reviving the Islamic Spirit" conference and others like it attract Muslim attendees by the tens of thousands. They feature major Islamic celebrity preachers who shape opinion and use rhetoric so hostile to non-Muslims – yet fully consistent with the doctrine – that, if expressed by non-Muslims, would be considered incitement.

What protects Tawhidi and similar figures from criticism by committed adherents is precisely the role they serve. They are the gleaming Trojan Horse that stands at the gate offering a beautiful gift – a face Westerners long to see, a voice telling them what they want to hear: that the cargo has nothing to do with the horse.

From a non-Muslim perspective, this is denial. By leading audiences away from the doctrine, figures like Tawhidi aid the Muslim Brotherhood's stated goal of destroying the West from within – "by their hands and the hands of the believers so that it is eliminated and Allah's deen is made victorious over all other deens." These "moderates" may even be actual members of the Brotherhood – there is really no way to know for sure.

- "إنه نوع من الجهاد الكبير في القضاء على الحضارة الغربية من الداخل ... وتخريب بيتها التعيس بأيديهم وأيدي المؤمنين حتى يتم القضاء عليها ويصبح دين الله منتصرا على سائر الأديان."
  (Muslim Brotherhood's Explanatory Memorandum1991)

The Brotherhood's core programme – Sharia supremacy, jihad, and enmity toward non-Muslims – is drawn directly from the Quran and Sunnah. Quran 9:29 commands fighting the People of the Book until they pay jizya and feel subdued. They have not invented these texts; they are core doctrine followed by Imam and jihadi alike. Focusing fire on the Brotherhood while protecting the doctrine is exactly what a Trojan Horse in denial does.

The Global Imams Council's "Symbols of Terror" guidebook, marketed as a tool for a "safer Canada," completes the picture. Presented as a neutral resource from an "apolitical" body following "mainstream Islamic teachings," it reassures politicians that "real imams" are on their side and that only certain symbols and organizations are the threat. Criticism rooted in the Quran, hadith, and classical fiqh can then be dismissed because the "global imams" have defined what counts as extremism.

Reliance on an 'insider' voice appears whenever a committee or commission is formed to examine Islamic violence: a Muslim member is expected, as though only an adherent can speak with authority, while the possibility that adherence itself precludes opposition to the doctrine is never considered.

They may be sincere, but sincerity is irrelevant to doctrine. Denial does not alter revelation. And it is pure hubris to believe that no such 'moderates' have preceded them. Fourteen centuries of them reaching out to those who greet them, each one welcomed, platformed, and held up as proof that the problem is not doctrinal but behavioural.

But the truth is unchanged. The horse carries the cargo. The cargo follows the doctrine. And the doctrine speaks for itself.

This pattern is not limited to polished Islamic presenters. It now includes a growing class of non-Muslims who have built entire careers analyzing "Islamism" while refusing to examine Islam itself. A video received from a former colleague features a prominent figure associated with the Institute for the Study of Global Antisemitism (ISGAP). His entire presentation is a perfect illustration of the Trojan Horse effect. He says the Muslim Brotherhood is a perversion of Islam. He insists that "good Muslims" respect democracy. He warns that Qatar and the

Brotherhood are not representative, while at the same time urging Western governments to partner with "reforming" Islamic countries like the UAE and Saudi Arabia. He describes Hamas as a branch of the Brotherhood, but never acknowledges that its goals are drawn directly from the Quran and hadith that all Muslims are required to follow. In short, he attacks the cargo while protecting the horse.

The false dichotomy between Islam and Islamism has become commonplace in Western political, academic and media discourse. Today it is almost taken for granted that Islam is a religion, while Islamism represents a modern political ideology that has somehow departed from or distorted it. Classical Islamic sources do not describe two separate systems. The Quran, hadith, Sira, and Sharia present Islam as a deen – a complete way of life – and most emphatically not merely a religion.

Which brings us to the question that most parliamentarians seem unwilling to ask: How can someone committed to Islam defend a Charter (or Constitution) whose principles contradict that doctrine at every level? This is particularly relevant for elected representatives and those entrusted with safeguarding non-Islamic states and their people.

My own experience illustrates how quickly that question is redirected away from doctrine and toward the person asking it. In response to a short post I had written about the Muslim slaughter of Christians in Nigeria, a Canadian counter-terrorism professional decided to make me the problem.

My article described decades of jihad against Nigerian Christians, the silence of Western churches, and the plain fact that Mohammed tied his own livelihood to jihad and war booty, just as the jihadis in Nigeria do today. I quoted Mohammed's own words, for example, his statement that he was shown 'the

East and the West, and given two treasures, the yellow and the white, meaning gold and silver' (Majah 3952). Mohammed himself declared: "My livelihood is under the shade of my spear, and he who disobeys my orders will be humiliated by paying jizya." (Bukhari, Book 56, Chapter 88). Nigeria is already at stage 3 of Islamization.

The West is still pretending it is not on the same path.

The response from this Canadian 'defender' – a self-described former 'jihadist extremist' who attended Quran school – was instructive. He wrote: "The ultimate irony is that the vast majority of Muslims don't believe these lies you are spreading but the terrorists and people like YOU, do! Stop pretending you're some kind of Crusader trying to make war with Islam as a whole. Muslims are 1/4 of the world's population. YOU'RE GONNA NEED A BIGGER BOAT!"

The reference to the Crusades is revealing. Like many Westerners, he invokes the term as a pejorative without acknowledging the centuries of jihad that preceded them. This is a passionate defence of Islam, not of Canada or its Charter, and certainly not of Christian Nigerians.

Islamic doctrine, including its view of jihad and Kafirs, is fundamentally at odds with the Canadian Charter's commitments to freedom of religion, equality before the law and equal protection. Yet a man tasked with counter-terrorism reflexively protects Islam from criticism, calls factual doctrinal citations "lies," and frames the critic as the threat. The same backlash is routinely directed at politicians who raise similar concerns. The Trojan Horse is not just at the gate. It is inside the security apparatus.

This same pattern of avoiding substantive engagement with doctrine while presenting a gentler face appears even in personal letters to critics. Recently, I received the following message from an anonymous sender: "Elaine, I mean this respectfully, but your analysis confuses the actions of extremists with the core teachings of the faith itself... The Arabic word Jihad does not mean 'holy war.' It means 'to strive' or 'to exert effort.' ... The Prophet Muhammad said: 'We have returned from the lesser jihad to the greater jihad.' ... The extremist cherry-picks and twists the doctrine to serve a political agenda. You accuse Muslims of presenting a 'rosy picture' of Islam, but in doing so, you present an equally incomplete and overly bleak one... Moreover, I welcome you to the message of Tawhid, and forgiveness, and Mercy from Allah. May Allah guide you, the way he guided Mary, and her son."

The message follows a familiar sequence. It begins with a claim of respect, immediately reframes the discussion away from the actual content of the work, invokes the fabricated "greater jihad" hadith (which has no reliable source in the canonical collections), selectively quotes verses about justice while ignoring the dualistic framework that allows either Meccan or Medinan verses to be deployed according to circumstance – conciliatory when weak, assertive when strong – accuses the critic of cherry-picking, and closes with an emotional and spiritual invitation that appropriates Christian figures. Notably, it does not address any of the specific doctrinal points raised. It simply relabels them as misunderstandings or extremism. This is dawa deployed not to inform, but to neutralize.

U.S., U.K., or Europe – the same pattern emerges.

Germany's AK Polis network runs prominent poster campaigns featuring supposed Muslims drinking alcohol ("I am a Muslim and I drink alcohol") or same-sex couples ("I am a Muslim") celebrating marriage. One such campaign appeared on large posters throughout Berlin and was distributed on postcards in over 300 restaurants, cultural venues, and cinemas, as well as on social media. It supported the first Day of Action against Islamophobia on March 15, 2026. Would AK Polis run similar commercials showing "I am Catholic and I had an abortion" to celebrate diversity? Of course not.

These campaigns promote behaviours that directly conflict with longstanding Islamic prohibitions on alcohol (Quran 5:90), same-sex relations (Quran 7:80–81), marriage to non-Muslims (Quran 2:221), and hijab (Quran 33:59, 24:31). Every child raised in a Muslim household knows these practices are not condoned under traditional teachings. Yet they are presented as evidence of successful integration. Earlier versions using non-Muslim models received thousands of threats, leading the organizers to switch to AI-generated images.

AK Polis describes itself as a cross-party network committed to protecting Germany's democratic order and opposing "political Islam." The problem with this framing is that it treats "political Islam" as a distortion rather than a direct expression of core doctrine. In Islamic teaching, religion and governance are not separate. The Quran repeatedly states that Islam is meant to prevail over all other systems (Quran 9:33, 48:28, 61:9). Mohammed functioned as prophet, lawgiver, military commander, and ruler. What is labelled "political Islam" is simply Islam operating according to its own foundational blueprint.

Support for these initiatives comes from small activist groups such as the Mernissi-de Gouges Organization and the Ibn Rushd-Goethe Mosque (founded by lawyer Seyran Ates), which promote mixed-gender prayer, female imams, and LGBTQ rights – positions widely rejected by traditional Islamic authorities. These organizations represent a fringe, not the mainstream. The

Ibn Rushd-Goethe Mosque has acknowledged the intense hostility these efforts provoke.

Islamic jurisprudence holds that a Muslim who knowingly engages in behaviour known to be haram has committed apostasy, for which the doctrine prescribes death (Bukhari 6922). The Quran also instructs Muslims not to take non-Muslims as allies except out of prudence (Quran 3:28).

Deceiving the public with such campaigns – whether driven by the Trojan Horses themselves or by desperate, ill-informed authorities eager for reassuring narratives – is not only disingenuous. It is dangerous. It misleads populations about the nature and scale of the threat, delaying necessary defences and ultimately risking lives and the future of entire societies.

This is not about individual people. Even if we work with a wonderful Muslim who is kind to dogs (also haram) and donates to charity (commendable if it is a Muslim charity), it changes nothing. The doctrine is the source of all jihad, stealth or violent. Mohammed himself made this clear:

- "There always will remain a group from my Ummah fighting upon the truth [Sharia], victorious over those who oppose them, until the last of them fight Al-Masih ad-Dajjal." (Dawud Vol.3, Bk 15, 2484)

In academic and policy discussions, researchers describe efforts to create a "Westernized" Muslim identity that minimizes visible Sharia. This is a fallacy. There is no radical Islam and no moderate Islam in the sense many hope for. There is only Islam. And no amount of campaigns from any source will ever change that.

One has only to look at the state of non-Islamic nations today – from Canada to Australia, from the United Kingdom to Germany and beyond – to recognize that decades of denial and accommodation have produced only abject failure.

This leaves society at a crossroads: continue down the path of denial and incremental surrender, or finally confront the doctrine honestly and defend the foundations of Western civilization.

5. A Civilization in Retreat

Western societies – once shaped by Enlightenment values and universal human rights – are increasingly choosing to privilege, appease, and even platform a 7th-century doctrinal system that is fundamentally incompatible with those values.

Because the West has come to regard Islam as a religion rather than a deen, institutions are vulnerable to capture. When authorities do not understand what they are dealing with, they cannot defend public space, education, and policy from the demands of Sharia. This has produced a pattern of accommodation that appears across multiple Western countries, with remarkably little resistance.

The Takeover of Public Space

One of the clearest signs of institutional capture and lack of resolve is the commandeering of public space. In parts of Paris, streets are regularly taken over for Islamic prayer with minimal intervention from authorities. A Reuters image from the Barbès / Goutte d'Or area in the 18th arrondissement shows a shop adjacent to a large group of Muslims engaged in salah – the Arabic term for prayer – blocking the road.

Islamic doctrine provides the justification. Ibn Kathir's tafsir on Quran 5:33 states that blocking roads is an act of making war. The commentary explains that "waging war" means to oppose or contradict Islam, and includes disbelief. Prescribed punishments include death, crucifixion, amputation, and exile. In this context, obstructing public roadways for salah is not a minor inconvenience but a political action that meets the Islamic definition of waging war.

Western authorities do not understand this doctrinal framing, yet they continue to seek advice from proponents of Islam who are permitted – and in some cases obligated – to mislead them if it benefits Islam. They imagine that banning certain organizations or passing symbolic legislation will contain the problem, but they do not recognise Sharia when they see it, and therefore cannot effectively regulate it. The result is the gradual surrender of public space without meaningful resistance.

Such incidents are occurring with increasing regularity and reflect a broader pattern in which Western institutions yield public space to Sharia while showing little will to stand by neutral rules that apply equally to all groups. Because the underlying doctrine is poorly understood – and because political leaders are reluctant to confront it directly – these takeovers continue.

The Infiltration of Secular Schools

The same pattern of institutional capture and lack of political will appears in secular education. In Quebec, a wave of school suspensions in 2024 triggered national headlines when it was revealed that some teachers were attempting to introduce Sharia concepts into the classroom. The controversy reopened long-standing debates about secularism and Sharia influence in French-speaking schools.

These teachers were not simply expressing personal belief. They were using their position within a public school system to prioritize the Islamic deen and enforce its rules over others – a clear example of creedist behaviour. Rather than maintaining neutrality, the administration allowed Sharia to enter the classroom under the assumption that all cultures are equally compatible with a secular school system.

This goes beyond individual failure. It reveals a deeper institutional failure to defend secular principles when they conflict with Islamic demands. Because authorities have misclassified Islam as a religion, they lack both the conceptual framework and the determination to recognize or resist its encroachment into public institutions. Instead, they open the door to it. The result is a gradual erosion of secular space, justified in the name of inclusion.

The same dynamic is visible in other French-speaking regions and across Europe. In many cases, authorities respond to Islamic demands in schools not with clear boundaries, but with further concessions – prayer rooms, dietary requirements, dress codes, and even curriculum adjustments – while showing little appetite to enforce consistent secular standards. This is not strength. It is institutional retreat.

The Reshaping of Public and Personal Space

Institutional capture is not limited to streets and schools. It also appears in official policy documents that seek to reshape public spaces to accommodate Sharia. A 2022 DEFRA (Department for Environment, Food & Rural Affairs) report on improving the ethnic diversity of visitors to England's protected landscapes is less about protected landscapes than about prioritising Sharia.

The inquiry explicitly excludes White British people from the category of "ethnic minorities," while directing policy changes around other groups. Its glossary defines protected landscapes through their contribution to national heritage but provides no equivalent consideration for Britain's indigenous population. The word "white" appears 51 times and "black" 117 times. Given that only around 67 million Britons are still of historic British and Irish stock – roughly 0.68% of humanity – the report's intense focus on changing their natural environment to suit others raises serious questions about whose heritage is being protected.

The demands highlighted are selective with the focus almost entirely on reshaping public space to facilitate the deen of Islam.

They do not insist on every rule, such as men growing beards or women remaining indoors. Instead, they target the areas that most effectively reshape the host society first – food, prayer facilities, toilets, and the presence of dogs in public spaces. These concerns are presented as barriers that must be addressed, with no parallel discussion of Christian, Hindu, Sikh, Jewish, Buddhist, or Bahá'í requirements anywhere in the document.

Particularly revealing is the treatment of dogs. In several places, the report highlights Muslim discomfort with dogs in public parks and protected landscapes. Dog ownership – a common and longstanding feature of British personal and public life – is presented as an obstacle to greater Muslim participation in these spaces. There is no equivalent discussion of how other groups might feel about any particular practice. The report effectively suggests that public space and even aspects of personal life (owning a dog) should be adjusted to suit Sharia.

- Mohammed said: 'We (Angles) do not enter a house in which there is a dog or a picture, The next day the Messenger of Allah commanded that all dogs be killed, even small dogs.' (an-Nasai 4276)

This is creedist deference in action. Sharia requirements are given priority in the reshaping of public and personal space, while all others – notably the host population – are ignored. It represents a further extension of institutional capture – moving beyond streets and schools into parks, leisure, and even private choices such as pet ownership. The fact that this appears in an official government-commissioned report demonstrates how deeply the pattern has embedded itself in policy-making, without resistance or even acknowledgement of what is occurring.

Accommodation Without Limits

Official reports and public consultations increasingly treat Sharia as non-negotiable demands that require accommodation, even when practical alternatives already exist within Islamic jurisprudence itself.

One participant in the DEFRA report explains the difficulty of preparing halal food in advance:

- "We require Halal food… it becomes more like sometimes a bit of a chore to make stuff before."

This is presented as a problem requiring institutional solutions. Yet Sharia already addresses such situations through the doctrine of darura (necessity), which permits Muslims to eat otherwise forbidden food when no halal alternative is reasonably available. The Quran itself states:

- "Whoever is compelled by necessity… there is no sin upon him." (Quran 2:173)

The report does not mention this flexibility. Instead, it frames Sharia as something that public institutions should actively facilitate. A pattern that appears repeatedly in policy discussions around education, healthcare, workplaces, and public spaces.

Each new privilege adds to a growing list of changes that Western institutions are expected to make. These demands extend beyond food and prayer into other areas of daily life, gradually reshaping what is considered normal in public and shared spaces.

Wudu in Public Facilities

Similar pressures appear around the use of public toilets and washing facilities. In several Western countries, there have been growing requests for dedicated spaces or modifications to allow Muslims to perform wudu (ritual washing before prayer) in schools, workplaces, airports, and other public buildings. These requests are typically framed as reasonable religious concessions.

What is not discussed is that these demands are no longer occasional or marginal. They stem from the Sharia requirement that Muslims maintain a state of ritual purity for the five daily prayers. While the Quran provides a basic outline of ablution (Quran 5:6), the detailed practice of wudu – including its frequency, the precise manner of performance, and the conditions that invalidate it – is derived primarily from the example and teachings of Mohammed. As the number of Muslims in a given institution grows, so do the practical demands on shared facilities. Over time, this creates pressure to redesign or allocate space specifically for Islamic ritual use.

Institutions rarely push back. Instead, they adjust – installing foot-washing stations, designating certain sinks for wudu, or creating separate prayer and washing areas. Each change is presented as inclusive and minor. Collectively, however, they represent another layer of institutional capture, in which public facilities are gradually modified to facilitate Sharia.

Pubs, Music, and the Haram Boundary

The pattern extends into areas of social and cultural life as well. In parts of Europe and the UK, there have been complaints from Muslim residents and activists about pubs, live music, and alcohol being served in certain neighbourhoods or near mosques. Grievances include noise, respect, or community standards.

From an Islamic doctrinal perspective, however, pubs and music or mixed-gender settings are not merely disliked – they are forbidden. Figures, paintings, and musical instruments have consistently been targeted as Jahiliyya – relics from the 'pre-Islamic period of ignorance.' The underlying issue is not simply one of cultural preference or noise complaints. It is Sharia.

- "Allah ordered me to do away with musical instruments flutes strings crucifixes and the affair of the 'pre-Islamic period of ignorance." (Reliance of the Traveller r40.1)
- "The bell is the musical instrument of Satan." (Muslim 2114)
- "Everything pertaining to the Days of Ignorance is under my feet completely abolished." (Muslim 1218a)

And for those who consider the wearing of silk, the drinking of alcoholic drinks and the use of musical instruments as lawful... "Allah will destroy them during the night and will let the mountain fall on them, and He will transform the rest of them into monkeys and pigs and they will remain so till the Day of Resurrection." (Bukhari 5590)

When institutions respond to these objections by restricting music, changing licensing rules, or discouraging certain venues, they are effectively allowing Sharia to influence public and commercial life. This creedism is rarely acknowledged openly. Instead, the changes are justified on other grounds – community harmony, noise control, or diversity. The result is the same: another area of normal Western social life is gradually restricted or reshaped to avoid offending the Islamic deen.

Expanding Institutional Demands

Perhaps the most visible and persistent demand is for dedicated prayer spaces. Schools, universities, hospitals, airports, public buildings, and workplaces are increasingly expected to provide rooms for Islamic prayer. These requests are almost always granted, with little if any discussion of whether equivalent facilities should be made available for other groups, or of the cost imposed on the institutions and taxpayers who fund them. Even where such rooms are initially described as multi-faith, they rarely remain so.

Over time, these incursions become normalised. What begins as a small concession can evolve into expectations of multiple daily prayer breaks, gender-separated spaces, and even calls to prayer being broadcast in or near public buildings. Each step is presented as reasonable and inclusive. Yet the combined result is a steady expansion of Sharia into spaces that were previously secular and shared.

This is not neutral policy. It is deference enabled by a fundamental misclassification of what Islam is, what it requires, and how it advances.

The result is predictable. Without a clear constitutional boundary around what qualifies as a protected religion, legislation aimed at restricting Sharia continues to fail. Privileges keep expanding – one prayer room, one halal cafeteria, one gender-segregated facility at a time – and the cumulative effect steadily alters the character of the nation, its civic structures, and its people.

- Quran 13:41 "Have they not seen that We set upon the land, reducing it from its borders? And Allah decides; there is no adjuster of His decision. And He is swift in account."

- Quran 21:43-44 Those who reject Allah have no protector against Us. They are unable to help themselves, nor can they be protected from Us. We have provided good things for these disbelievers and their fathers until life was prolonged for them. Do they not see

> that We set upon the land, reducing it from its borders? How, then, can they expect to overcome?

Western authorities continue down this path not because they have carefully weighed the doctrinal implications, but because they lack both the knowledge and the willingness to do otherwise. They follow guides who assure them that these adjustments are harmless, temporary, or even enriching – while the underlying pattern of institutional capture continues unchecked.

Social welfare systems have become an unintended source of funding for Islamic expansion. In multiple countries, individuals and networks have used social benefits, student loans, and disability payments to support full-time dawa, mosque activity, and in some cases travel to conflict zones (Ellinger 2025). Classical jurisprudence does not regard taxes paid to non-Muslim rulers as a legitimate obligation; some scholars treat the description of such taxes as a "right" as itself reprehensible (Reliance of the Traveller r12). The reverse flow – non-Muslims supporting Muslims – is doctrinally closer to the model of jizya. The result is that public funds intended for social support are redirected, often invisibly, into the strengthening of a parallel system that does not accept the legitimacy of the host society's legal and fiscal order.

But at what point does facilitating Sharia irrevocably change the established character of public life? Because Western institutions have misclassified Islam as simply another religion, they are unable to draw that line. Instead, they continue to follow those who present each new demand as uncontroversial, while the slow transformation of the state and its agencies proceeds largely without a brake pedal and without a solution.

And just as Mohammed's example is accepted as authoritative for ritual demands such as wudu, consistency requires acknowledging that the same body of sources also records his campaigns, orders, and personal responsibility for the killing of those who refused submission to Islam. Western societies currently choose which parts of that example to honour. When the balance of numbers and authority changes, that choice will no longer rest with the host society.

Voices That Matter

In this environment, those who resist the advance of Islam face immediate and expected condemnation. This is why politicians who want to defend the freedoms their constitutions promise should understand that they do not need to become experts on Sharia.

They need only stand firmly on the platform of universal human rights – rights that classical Islamic doctrine systematically denies. That single stance is enough to open the door to a legislative solution: requiring any belief system that seeks protected status and public privileges to demonstrate consistency with the constitution. Private belief remains untouched. What the state chooses to reward, however, must serve the state's own foundations. There is a clear difference.

Against this backdrop, an increasing number of politicians have chosen to push back. When they speak plainly about Islamic doctrine, the condemnation is usually swift and personal. Two examples illustrate the pattern.

In Australia, Senator Pauline Hanson asked a simple question: "Are there any good Muslims?" The outrage was immediate. But it is worth examining what the word "good" actually means in this context (see Glossary).

In Islamic doctrine, "good" is not determined by human reason or universal ethics. It is defined by obedience to Sharia. Classical Islamic law is explicit on this point:

- "The good is not what reason considers good... The measure of good and bad, according to this school of thought, is the Sacred Law, not reason." (Reliance of the Traveller a1.4)

The Quran reinforces the same mentality:

- "Fighting is prescribed for you... it may be that you dislike a thing which is good for you... but Allah knows and you know not." (Quran 2:216)
- "Then We put you (O Muhammad) on a clear way of command [Sharia]. So follow it, and do not follow the desires of those who do not know." (Quran 45:18)

For Islam, a "good" Muslim is one who submits to Sharia. Under Western constitutional principles, a good citizen is one who upholds equality before the law and respects the rights of others regardless of their belief, or sex. These are not minor differences in emphasis. They are incompatible definitions.

The same tension surfaced in the United States when Congressman Randy Fine responded to a statement from an Islamic activist supporting the new Mayor of New York. The activist had written that dogs "definitely have a place in society, just not as indoor pets," adding, "Finally, NYC is coming to Islam."

Fine replied: "If they force us to choose, the choice between dogs and Muslims is not a difficult one."

The backlash was predictable. The Council on American-Islamic Relations (CAIR) and various political figures condemned him, framing his comment as bigotry. What they did not address was the doctrinal basis for the original statement. Islamic sources are clear on the status of dogs:

Mohammed ordered that dogs be killed, later making an exception only for hunting and herding dogs. Black dogs were described as devils (Tirmidhi 338). He also stated that when a dog licks a vessel, it must be washed seven times and rubbed with earth the eighth time (Muslim 280a). In today's halal production sanitation standards, contamination by dogs is classified as najas – severe impurity – requiring precisely that purification ritual (Abdullah).

- Remove the contaminant and wash seven times with running water, one of which shall be with water mixed with soil. The first wash shall clear the najs. The water from first cleaning shall not remain behind and the successive wash shall be counted as the second wash. The amount of soil used is just enough to make a suspension.

The same terminology that deems dogs impure also classifies unbelievers as impure:

- "O you who believe! Verily, the Mushrikun [unbelievers] are najasun (impure)." (Quran 9:28)

- "When one fears ...that a non-Muslim may touch it [the Quran], or that it may come into contact with some filth, then one must pick it up if there is no safe place for it..." (Reliance of the Traveller e8.3)

When politicians who simply acknowledge these teachings are condemned – even by those who claim to oppose Sharia – it reveals a deeper problem. Leaders do not need to become experts on Islamic doctrine. They do, however, need to acknowledge that a serious problem exists and requires a solution. Instead, many Western leaders attack anyone who speaks about the content of the doctrine. Some are so uninformed that they do not even connect Sharia with the doctrine itself, having accepted the claim that Mohammed and the primary sources are solely about peace and love. They are unwilling to confront the reality.

This pattern of relying on incomplete information is not new. In the 18th century, Thomas Jefferson owned a copy of the Quran and argued that "Mahometans" should not be excluded from civil rights. At the time, civil rights referred to property ownership, access to courts, and personal liberty. Jefferson had no access to the hadith collections or classical Sharia manuals that later supplied the detailed rules and legal structure through which Quranic verses are applied as a comprehensive system of law and governance. Using his limited 18th-century knowledge to justify modern state-approved Islamic schools, Sharia arbitration, or parallel legal authority makes little constitutional sense.

Accommodation is not reciprocated in Islamic countries because Islamic doctrine rejects the very idea of competing legal and moral systems as equally legitimate. It demands supremacy: its own system is the only one that has the right to govern. Where full implementation is not possible and cannot be attained, the texts direct believers to emigrate to lands where it can be advanced:

- "Was not the earth of Allah spacious [enough] for you to emigrate therein?" (Quran 4:97)

There are already fifty-seven OIC member states in which Sharia shapes, or is expected to shape, law to varying degrees. Western constitutional systems rest on voluntary belief, equal protection, and the separation of religion from law. A doctrine that mandates legal hierarchy, supremacy of the deen, and the subordination of non-Muslims cannot coexist with those principles without eroding them over time.

Acknowledging reality is not bigotry.

The real issue is a political culture that has refused to confront what Islamic doctrine actually requires while continuing to accede to its demands. Confronting doctrine honestly is essential if constitutional societies are to defend their foundations instead of surrendering them piece by piece.

Sharia in America: Doctrine vs. Denial

A congressional subcommittee hearing on Sharia in America in February 2026 illustrated this conflict sharply. Witnesses presented Sharia directly from authoritative Islamic legal texts and manuals: a comprehensive system regulating law, warfare, social order, family relations, punishment, and expansion. One that demands obedience. They cited classical jurisprudence defining jihad as war against non-Muslims – a communal obligation aimed at making Islam prevail over all other ways of life (Quran 9:33).

- "It is He who has sent His Messenger with guidance and the deen of truth to manifest it over all deen." (Quran 9:33)

They described existing Sharia tribunals operating in family and civil matters in the U.S. and Europe, displacing Western standards on custody, equality, and consent. And they documented the steady proliferation of mosques, nonprofits, schools, and Sharia-compliant finance. One witness detailed how foreign legal judgments and religious arbitration are already entering Western courts through treaty and contract mechanisms, particularly in family law, where custody and consent standards diverge sharply from constitutional norms. Another described the scale of institutional growth in a single state: hundreds of mosques, hundreds of Islamic nonprofits, Sharia-compliant finance, and billions in public funds directed to Islamic entities in recent years, alongside open advocacy for Islamic theocracy over democracy and the appearance of Sharia patrols and informal enforcement.

The counter-response from some politicians revealed the more fundamental problem: a refusal to listen to those who actually know the doctrine and oppose it. The witnesses were non-Muslims who had studied the primary sources and placed them on the record. Instead of engaging that evidence, Sharia was repeatedly reframed as nothing more than personal religious observance – comparable to Jewish halakha or Christian canon law. Concern about its legal and political dimensions was dismissed as prejudice or political opportunism. One member of Congress openly admitted he did not know what Sharia was but had done a quick Google search prior to the conference. He then proceeded to defend it under the undefined category of religion. Others treated the hearing itself as illegitimate, accusing those who raised doctrinal concerns of demonizing Muslims for political gain, invoking moral equivalence with other extremisms, and attempting to discredit witnesses personally rather than address the texts they had cited. The pattern was consistent: avoid the doctrine, attack the premise of the hearing, and treat any examination of Islamic law as beyond the bounds of acceptable discussion. Institutional creedism on full display.

The hearing thus exposed a recurring pattern: on one side, well-informed non-Muslim voices calling out a doctrinal system that asserts supremacy and comprehensive authority; on the other, a political culture determined to reduce it to harmless private piety. This minimization allows continued deference to Sharia while avoiding any serious legal or cultural defence of secular constitutional rights and freedoms. The information was available and was entered into the record. The refusal was not a lack of evidence. It was a lack of political will.

Western societies continue to underestimate Islam – treating it as a religion that can be accommodated rather than as a civilizational system that does not accommodate them.

PART III: CORRECTION

One indication of how deeply the Deen Fallacy has become embedded is that modern artificial intelligence systems also default to rendering deen as "religion." This is not because the software has independently concluded that "religion" is the most accurate equivalent. Modern translation systems, including Google Translate, DeepL, and many other AI-powered language tools learn from billions of existing human translations and bilingual texts. Because deen has routinely been rendered as "religion" for well over a century in English translations of Islamic literature, dictionaries, and academic works, the system simply reproduces that usage. In other words, it reflects the accumulated errors of earlier work rather than making an independent linguistic or theological judgment. The result is that a translation choice made generations ago is continually reinforced by modern technology, giving the appearance of objective confirmation when it is, in reality, the repetition of an inherited convention.

1. Why Reactive Measures Fail

Meaningful solutions begin with accurate definitions. A problem that has been incorrectly described cannot be effectively addressed, no matter how sincere the effort. The pattern of denial, accommodation, and recurring policy failure documented in the preceding chapters stems in large part from a fundamental misclassification of Islam – not as a deen, but as a religion in the Western sense. Correcting that misunderstanding requires more than new policies. It requires applying the same standards of analysis to Islamic doctrine that are routinely applied to other comprehensive systems of law and governance.

Why Bills Banning Sharia Will Fail

In June 2017, Texas enacted House Bill 45, known as American Laws for American Courts that prohibits Texas courts from applying any foreign law – including Sharia – in family or contractual disputes. And yet Texas is overrun with Sharia that is advancing on multiple fronts.

In September of 2025, a Florida Congressional Representative proposed U.S. legislation, H.R. 5512, titled the 'No Shari'a Act'. It promised to prohibit U.S. courts from enforcing any ruling "based in whole or in part" on Sharia if it violated constitutional rights.

The bill was well-intentioned but doomed. Remarkably, it never once defines the word "Sharia" – leaving judges to guess what qualifies. Without that definition, and without fixing the deeper constitutional blind spot on what actually counts as a protected "religion," the legislation is unenforceable and, frankly, meaningless.

The bill's main provisions simply restated what American courts already do. They prohibit enforcement of judgments that rely on Sharia or foreign law if those judgments violate constitutional rights, and they place similar restrictions on contracts and family law matters. All of this is already within the existing authority of American courts.

The real problem is that the U.S. Constitution does not establish a threshold for public advantage. It protects the free exercise of religion, but nowhere does it define what qualifies. This omission is now being ruthlessly exploited. The West is effectively subsidizing its own submission by extending legal protection and public privilege to a doctrine that rejects the very freedoms upon which those protections are founded.

Sharia is not a set of private beliefs. It is an all-encompassing socio-economic-political and military system that has been in force for fourteen centuries and is now expanding westward. It regulates criminal law, contracts, warfare, taxation, speech, inheritance, dress, sexuality, marriage, and much more. Islam classifies the world into Muslims and non-Muslims and mandates different legal rules and treatment for each. Yet under current U.S. law, Sharia is treated as a protected religious expression – a fatal misunderstanding

Quran 45:18 defines Sharia explicitly:

- "Then We put you, [O Muhammad], on an ordained way [Arabic: shari'a] concerning the deen; so follow it and do not follow the desires of those who do not know."

Sharia is the commanded path, the ordained way. It is Islam itself, not a human interpretation or external add-on. Attempts to separate "Islam" from "Sharia" misunderstand the foundational texts. Any law claiming to ban "Sharia" while still protecting "Islam" is attempting the impossible. The two are doctrinally inseparable.

Bills of this kind are unlikely to prevent workplace prayer breaks, gender-segregated events, halal marketing that raises zakat, or Sharia-compliant finance. They are also unlikely to restrict Islamic schools from teaching that Jews and Christians are cursed, or to prevent the development of private Islamic communities organized around Sharia-compliant living. None of these practices clearly violate constitutional rights under current interpretations, yet all of them represent expressions of Sharia that are steadily reshaping aspects of American life on behalf of the Islamic ummah – a nation without borders.

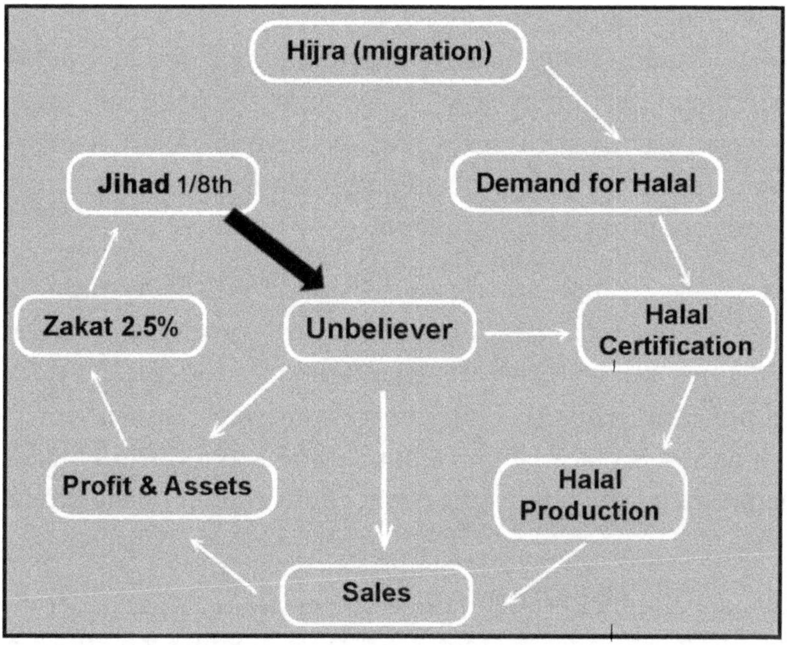

Such legislation would also have had little effect on the political transformation of cities like Dearborn, Michigan. That shift occurred through entirely legal channels – immigration, electoral organizing, and the routine granting of religious concessions.

Dearborn's Muslim-majority city council operates under Michigan law, not Sharia courts, yet many of its policy priorities (amplifying the adhan over loudspeakers, honorary street naming for figures who have praised jihadist groups) flow directly from mainstream Islamic doctrinal positions that would be unthinkable in a secular or Christian-majority city of similar size. There are many such examples.

The same legislation would also fail to prevent creedist developments such as EPIC City, also known as Epic Ranch, in Texas – a planned Muslim-centric community designed around Sharia-compliant amenities, including a central mosque, halal retail, and interest-free but not cost-free financing (Saleem). It would likewise have no effect on projects such as the "New Africa" Islamic residential development approved by the Little Rock Planning Commission in December 2020. That six-acre project currently includes twenty-two single-family homes, an Islamic school, two mosques, and a clinic, in addition to the already operating Huda Academy.

Buyers are required to sign an "Islamic Bill of Assurance," a private covenant that mandates conformity to Quranic guidelines on architecture, maintenance, the prohibition of alcohol and thus is inherently creedist. Control of the community is placed under a homeowners association linked to the mosque, which retains permanent oversight of the property rules.

Both developments, like many others across the country, are entirely legal under current First Amendment protections and property law. They have been approved and advanced because of a fundamental misclassification of Islam as a religion, rather than a deen. Islam is not merely a system of personal belief. It is a civilizational entity with its own comprehensive legal, social, and political order. As long as that distinction remains unrecognized in law and policy, such projects will continue to receive the same protections and concessions granted to ordinary religious communities.

This is hardly unprecedented. As this book has shown, throughout history, commercial, diplomatic, political, and even academic institutions have repeatedly chosen to set aside fundamental differences in values and human rights whenever convenience, profit, influence, or strategic advantage was at stake.

Just as Queen Elizabeth I set aside both the earlier conquest of Christian lands and the ongoing practices of the Ottoman Empire – slavery, the killing of apostates, female genital mutilation, and judicial amputations – while still calling herself the defender of the Christian faith in order to pursue trade and commerce, Western governments do the same today. Known current practices such as FGM, the death penalty for apostasy, amputations, and slavery itself are overlooked. Political expediency, trade, and commercial advantage once again take priority, while the deen continues to advance.

The same calculation continues. Governments and corporations downplay or ignore profound differences in principles – particularly regarding individual rights, equality, and the treatment of non-Muslims and women – in pursuit of trade, investment, and political influence. The justifications change with the era, but the underlying willingness to subordinate principle to expediency remains remarkably consistent.

Stopping Sharia Requires More Than Prohibition

People often say that Sharia must be outlawed, yet few recognize what they are actually asking to prohibit. Sharia is not merely a formal legal code that operates in courts. It is a comprehensive system of behaviour, authority, and obligation rooted in doctrine and regarded by believers as divine law – superior to any man-made constitution. Where Sharia and constitutional principles come into conflict, the former is treated as binding.

This is already visible in the sharp rise in violence against women following large-scale migration from Islamic countries – much of it driven by creedist attitudes toward non-Muslims and unveiled women. It also appears in forced marriages, in the social and familial punishment of those who leave Islam, and in the enforcement of Sharia norms on Muslims who would prefer not to comply but have not left it for fear of retribution or for other reasons.

Sharia is already operating in parallel with, and in many cases above, constitutional law. Sharia councils function across multiple Western countries, settling matters of inheritance and testimony according to Islamic rules that treat women and non-Muslims unequally. Islamic centres – many of them in receipt of government funding – routinely conduct both civil and Islamic marriages and offer Islamic studies classes for youth. These arrangements expand quietly, largely unseen by legislators and rarely challenged, while constitutional guarantees of equal treatment are steadily eroded for those caught within them.

As Islamic populations grow and political influence expands, the pressure to support Sharia intensifies, as evidenced by campaigns to legalize cousin marriage in the United Kingdom and by the continued practice and legal defence of female genital mutilation in Western countries. In each case, constitutional protections are being overridden in practice long before they are challenged in law.

Neutralizing Sharia therefore requires more than prohibiting organizations or isolated practices. Because it operates through an integrated system of doctrine, institutions, and social obligations, attempts to outlaw Sharia itself produce little more than confusion, expensive litigation, and the continued expansion of parallel norms beneath the surface of constitutional systems outside the Islamic world.

Freedom Requires Law

A belief system that upholds slavery, polygamy, wife-beating, child marriage, apostasy laws, and parallel legal structures should not receive the same legal protections as one rooted in peace, equality, and human dignity. That much should be obvious.

Freedom is not preserved by tolerance. It is preserved by law. And today, the law in most Western democracies is too vague about what qualifies as a "religion" deserving of special status, tax exemption, charitable recognition, or legal protection.

This vagueness has allowed a supremacist ideology in the robes of religion to claim and exploit rights it systematically denies to others. Western legal systems remain structurally ill-equipped to address this reality. When courts are forbidden to examine religion – which they are – there is only one lawful path forward: establishing a clear threshold. If a belief system wants public benefits, it must meet public standards.

What kind of standards? At minimum, equality before the law, freedom of religion, respect for the rights of children, women, and non-members, and rejection of violence and coercion.

Western governments have already shown that protection is not absolute. Pre-1960s American courts (Reynolds v. United States (1879), Davis v. Beason (1890), The Late Corporation of the Church of Jesus Christ of Latter-Day Saints v. United States (1890)) and current European jurisprudence (Refah Partisi v. Turkey (2003) and Dogru v. France (2008)) recognize that a belief system may be denied legal recognition, institutional or public privilege where its authoritative doctrines conflict with fundamental constitutional principles.

On a personal level, every time we say, hear, read, or write the word "religion" in connection with Islam, we reinforce a fundamental error in thinking. One of the simplest and most powerful things individuals can do is to start using the correct terminology. Use the word deen to describe Islam. When people ask "What is a deen?", take the opportunity to explain. Over time, this small shift in language can elevate the entire conversation and help correct a misclassification that has shaped policy for generations. Learn to call out creedism just as one would call out racism.

On a national level, the solution is legislation. The final section of this book offers a clear, enforceable legal path forward. It relies on a universal standard rooted in human rights and does not target any belief by name – only a requirement to meet agreed principles. This is how we protect real freedom of belief while denying cover to ideologies that exploit it.

This approach does not prohibit belief. It protects the freedom to believe while refusing to reward those that utilize constitutional freedoms to violate the rights of others.

Without this, Islam will continue advancing one accommodation at a time, protected by the very constitutional freedoms that Sharia seeks to restrict or replace.

The Benefits of Correct Classification

Western institutions, even those with strong secular traditions such as France's laïcité, must acknowledge that Islam compels conduct, governance, and legal authority, not merely private belief. In practice, Islamic influence advances through multiple channels – cultural associations, educational programs, halal certification bodies, foreign-funded organizations, and demands framed as "cultural rights." Whatever label is used, the deen seeks institutional concessions and eventual supremacy. Continuing to facilitate its expansion is inimical to the future of constitutional government across the non-Islamic world.

Islam, through Sharia, directly contravenes core principles of equality, freedom of speech, freedom of religion, and the supremacy of secular law. Addressing that reality does not undermine liberty – it restores it.

The practical consequences are significant.

Legislative reform will transform public awareness in a way that nothing else can. Decades of misclassification, apologetics, propaganda, and dawah will give way to informed public discussion based upon objective evidence rather than inherited assumptions.

Once Islam is classified under the statutory threshold as a belief system that does not qualify for the legal status of religion, that classification applies generally. It is not open to challenge by individual organizations, mosques, charities, schools, or advocacy groups. The designation is statutory, not adjudicative. Thousands of organizations cannot litigate it away one case at a time.

The protected status that has enabled Islam to obtain public funding, charitable status, tax advantages, educational accreditation, institutional partnerships, and countless other public benefits will therefore no longer be available simply because Islam has been misclassified as a religion. Claims for religious accommodation, parallel legal systems, faith-based exemptions, foreign-funded influence operations, preferential consultation with self-appointed representatives, or special access to public institutions such as schools, prisons, the military, and hospitals will no longer flow automatically from the assertion that Islam is a religion. The same principle will apply to immigration, refugee determination, charitable regulation, Islamic finance, and every other area in which public benefits or institutional recognition are sought.

Public privilege will no longer rest upon mistranslation, misclassification, or political pressure, but upon objective constitutional principles applied equally to everyone. The result is not the restriction of belief, but the correction of a longstanding legal misclassification. Constitutional protections remain. Automatic public privilege will not.

2. Correcting the Legal Classification

A Practical Path Forward

This book has argued that the West's greatest error has not been misunderstanding a single word, but misclassifying an entire system.

History already supplies a clear precedent. Before Utah was admitted to the Union, the United States required the formal abandonment of polygamy as a condition of statehood. The issue was never private belief. It was whether legal institutions seeking public recognition could remain incompatible with constitutional principles. Public recognition was made contingent upon conformity with those principles. Islam, by contrast, cannot abandon Sharia without abandoning the deen itself.

For generations, Western legal systems have extended the protections and privileges associated with religion to Islam on the assumption that it belongs within that category. That assumption is mistaken. Islam is a deen – a comprehensive system of law, governance, and way of life that includes religion but is not limited to it. The Quran itself states the objective: "It is He who has sent His Messenger with guidance and the deen of truth to make it prevail over all other deens..." (Quran 9:33).

When a legal classification is wrong at its foundation, the advantages that rest upon it have no proper basis. The remedy is not endless litigation or political discretion. It is to correct the classification upon which those decisions rest.

Correcting the classification is not a call to strip recognition from religion. What has traditionally been understood as religion – systems centred on belief, worship, and personal conduct – poses no structural challenge to constitutional order.

The deen of Islam is different. It advances through law, politics, finance, education, and governance. A uniform withdrawal of religious privileges therefore changes nothing, as French laïcité has shown; the system continues under other forms. Only an accurate legal definition – one that distinguishes a comprehensive civilizational order from what has traditionally been understood as religion – allows the state to draw the necessary boundary and protect future generations from repeating the same error.

Legislatures routinely define legal categories that confer recognition, privilege, or public benefits. They determine what qualifies as a corporation, a charity, an educational institution, a legal or biological parent. Once those definitions are established in law, they apply generally and consistently. Courts are not expected to determine the meaning of those terms afresh in every individual case. The same principle must apply here.

The law cannot determine what religion is in any philosophical or theological sense, nor is that its purpose. Its role is simply to establish an objective constitutional qualification standard governing eligibility for legal recognition and the public benefits that accompany that status. Those qualifications must be consistent with the Constitution, the rule of law, and the fundamental rights and freedoms upon which democratic societies are founded.

Belief systems that meet the statutory qualifications become eligible for the benefits attached to that status. Those that do not, do not. This does not infringe upon personal belief, which is all that is constitutionally guaranteed. Individual constitutional freedoms remain fully protected.

To qualify for legal recognition that conveys with it public privileges, a belief system must demonstrably affirm – in its foundational texts and authoritative jurisprudence – equality before the law, including in matters of testimony, inheritance, and divorce; reject violence or coercion in the enforcement of belief; reject slavery, polygamy, and female genital mutilation as religious rights; protect children and the freedom to leave the faith; and recognize the supremacy of civil law over any competing legal code. A simple public profession of compatibility is insufficient.

Organizations established under a particular belief system can not determine or redefine the category under which they fall; they inherit the legal consequences of the statutory classification established by law. Nor may those consequences be avoided simply by adopting another label. An organization describing itself as cultural, educational, humanitarian, or by any other designation remains subject to the legal classification of the belief system under which it is constituted.

This principle is equally applicable in jurisdictions such as France. Under *laïcité*, the State neither recognizes nor favours religion in the manner common to some other democracies. The same statutory qualification standard can therefore be applied to determine eligibility for whatever legal recognition, accommodation, or public benefits French law may provide, while preserving both freedom of belief and the constitutional principle of state neutrality.

The complete Threshold Proposition, together with model legislation prepared for multiple jurisdictions and a Guide to Adjudication, is presented in A Civilizational Reckoning: Understanding the Threat, Reclaiming the Future (Ellinger 2025). Those materials provide a practical framework through which legislatures, governments and courts may implement these principles within their own constitutional traditions. As a convenience to the reader, the Guide to Adjudication is also provided as an Appendix to this book.

No democratic society can long preserve freedom if it lacks the legal language to distinguish between private belief and systems that seek public authority, legal privilege, or constitutional supremacy. The West's error began with a mistranslation that produced a misclassification. Correcting that classification does not predetermine political decisions or judicial outcomes. It simply restores the ability of constitutional democracies to apply their own principles clearly, consistently and equally to all.

The law cannot protect what it has first failed to define. Correct classification is therefore not the end of the conversation. It is the indispensable foundation upon which every lasting solution must rest.

Appendix A: Guide to Adjudication

Doctrinal Clarification – For Use in Assessing Eligibility

Purpose of This Appendix

This appendix is not a declaration of judgment. It is a factual clarification intended to support legal analysis when conflicts arise between a doctrine's claims and its practices. In legal systems where courts are prohibited from assessing religious content, this evidentiary clarification provides a framework for understanding Islamic doctrine's internal logic, especially where deception, contradiction, and dual standards are permitted or mandated. Its purpose is to aid lawmakers and officials in evaluating eligibility for legal privileges – not to predetermine that Islam or any other system fails to meet the legal threshold. That determination must be made independently, through duly enacted legislation or judicial review.

---

1. Doctrinal Deception: Taqiyya, Kitman, Tauriya

Islamic jurisprudence contains provisions that permit or encourage deceit under certain circumstances, especially toward Non-Muslims (Kafirs). These include:

- Taqiyya – Doctrinal permission to lie or deceive when necessary to achieve a permissible goal under Islamic law. This includes protecting Islam, avoiding harm, reconciling parties, or securing advantage. Lying is not inherently sinful if the purpose is sanctioned and benefits Islam. There are many doctrinally affirmed variations.

- Quran 3:28; 16:106; see also Tafsir Ibn Kathir on 3:28
- Kitman – Lying by omission or silence, concealing part of the truth while appearing truthful.
- Tauriya – Intentionally misleading through ambiguous or double-meaning statements. Supported in Islamic legal manuals including *Reliance of the Traveller* r10 and r8.2, which states:
  "Speaking is a means to achieve objectives. If a permissible aim is attainable through both telling the truth and lying, it is unlawful to accomplish through lying... and obligatory to lie if the goal is obligatory."
  "But it is religiously precautionary not to lie but rather to employ words that give a misleading impression."

Implication: When doctrine allows strategic misrepresentation, external statements by Islamic organizations or individuals cannot always be taken at face value. This significantly complicates the task of assessing alignment with legal norms such as truthfulness, transparency, and good faith.

---

2. Abrogation (Naskh): Later Verses Override Earlier Ones

In Islamic doctrine, abrogation is the principle that later revelations supersede earlier ones (Quran 2:106). While some early verses of the Quran are peaceful or conciliatory, many of these have been abrogated by later verses commanding warfare, inequality, or discrimination.

Examples:

- Peaceful verse (early):
  "There is no compulsion in religion..." (Quran 2:256)
  Abrogated by later verses:
  "Fight those who do not believe in Allah..." (Quran 9:29)
  "When the sacred months have passed, kill the polytheists wherever you find them..." (Quran 9:5)

As per Tafsir Ibn Kathir on Quran 9:5:

"This was the Ayah of the Sword which abrogated every agreement of peace between the Prophet and any idolater."

Implication: Claims of peaceful doctrine based on early verses must be weighed against the doctrinal supremacy of later commands. Without understanding abrogation, Non-Muslim evaluators may mistakenly believe that contradictory doctrines are coequal, when in fact the more violent or supremacist verses are legally binding under Sharia.

---

3. Dual Standards: One Law for Muslims, Another for non-Muslims

Islamic doctrine establishes dual moral and legal standards:

- For Muslims: Brotherhood, legal privilege, and internal solidarity (Quran 49:10).
- For non-Muslims: Hostility, inequality, and subjugation (Quran 98:6; 8:55; 3:110; 9:29).
  Ibn Kathir on 98:6 confirms: "They are the worst of creatures."

Under Sharia:

- A Muslim may not be executed for killing a Kafir (ROT o1.2(2)).
- Testimony of a Non-Muslim is generally not accepted against a Muslim in Islamic courts (Reliance, o24.7).
- Jizya tax, subjugation and humiliation are imposed on Non-Muslims (Quran 9:29).

Implication: The appearance of universality in some teachings must be evaluated in context. Legal and ethical obligations differ significantly depending on whether the subject is Muslim or Non-Muslim. Systems that promote legal inequality based on belief cannot meet the threshold of universal human rights.

---

4. Contradictory Rules Coexist in Islamic Law

Islamic doctrine does not follow Western unitary logic, where contradictory propositions cannot both be true. Instead, Islamic jurisprudence permits contextual contradiction:

- Peace and war both apply – depending on time, place, and strength.
- Truth and deception both apply – depending on audience and objective.
- Equality and inequality both apply – depending on who is being addressed.

The Sunnah of Mohammed likewise shows shifting strategies:

- Early Meccan years: preaching, persuasion.
- Later Medinan years: conquest, enforcement, and lawmaking.

Implication: Apparent contradictions in doctrine are not errors – they are strategic. Evaluators must therefore examine which rules are active in which contexts, especially when assessing eligibility for legal privilege.

---

5. Why This Appendix Matters

This appendix is intended as an evidentiary aid for legislatures, legal analysts, and policymakers. It does not declare that Islam fails the legal test for religious protection. Rather, it highlights why Islam is a special case requiring deeper scrutiny.

Where contradictions exist between doctrinal texts and public claims, the burden of clarification must lie with those seeking recognition, but the evaluation itself must be independently adjudicated. A system that claims to affirm universal rights while permitting exceptions through abrogation or dual standards cannot be assumed to meet a rights-based threshold without detailed examination conducted by those outside the doctrine.

---

6. Conflicted Allegiance and the Supremacy of Sharia

Islamic doctrine establishes that allegiance to Allah's law (Sharia) supersedes any earthly legal system. This is not merely theological – it has legal and political consequences:

- Quran 5:44 – "Whoever does not judge by what Allah has revealed – then it is they who are the disbelievers."

- Quran 33:36 – "It is not for a believing man or a believing woman, when Allah and His Messenger have decided a matter, to have any choice in their affair."

These verses establish that Muslims are doctrinally obligated to obey divine law above any man-made system. Even citizenship oaths, parliamentary votes, or public duties may be considered subordinate to Sharia.

In practice, this can create conflicted allegiance:

- Muslim judges, legislators, law enforcement, or school administrators may face doctrinal conflict when enforcing civil law that contradicts Sharia.
- Islamic scholars or leaders applying for charitable status or public funding may interpret their commitments through a Sharia-first lens, regardless of their public assurances.

Implication: Systems that explicitly or implicitly require believers to disobey civil law in favour of divine law present a structural conflict with constitutional order. Legal recognition or funding of such systems must account for this inherent allegiance gap.

This is not prejudice. It is due diligence.

---

7. Emigration Is Doctrinally Prescribed When Sharia Cannot Be Fulfilled

Islamic doctrine obligates Muslims to emigrate (make *hijrah*) if they are unable to fully implement or live by Sharia law. This principle is made explicit in *Quran 4:97*:

- "Indeed, those whom the angels take [in death] while wronging themselves – [the angels] will say, 'In what [condition] were you?' They will say, 'We were oppressed in the land.' The angels will say, 'Was not the earth of Allah spacious [enough] for you to emigrate therein?'"

Tafsir Ibn Kathir confirms that this ayah applies to Muslims who remained among disbelievers when they were able to leave, noting that their failure to emigrate meant they were "wronging themselves."

In practical terms, Muslims who regard the full implementation of Sharia – including its stated doctrinal objective of global submission to Islam – as a binding religious duty, and who find themselves unable to fulfil this duty within a non-Islamic legal framework, are doctrinally instructed to emigrate.

- "It is He who sent His Messenger with guidance and the deen of truth to manifest it over all deen. And sufficient is Allah as Witness." (Quran 9:33, 48:28, 61:9)

Quran 4:97 rebukes those who remain in lands where they cannot implement Islam, and this constitutes a doctrinal exit clause for committed adherents. Given this doctrinal provision, legal restrictions on the enforcement or public funding of Sharia in the West cannot be construed as persecution. They are lawful acts of constitutional self-preservation – anticipated and provided for within Islamic doctrine itself.

Bibliography

Foundational Islamic Texts and Translations

al-Ṭabarī, The History of al-Ṭabarī, Vol. 6: Muḥammad at Mecca, trans. Montgomery Watt and M. V. McDonald (SUNY Press, 1988).

al-Ṭabarī, Tafsīr (Jāmiʿ al-bayān), ed. Aḥmad Muḥammad Shākir (Cairo: Dār al-Maʿārif), Q 66:1.

Ali, Abdullah Yusuf. The Meaning of the Holy Quran. Amana Publications, 2001.

Bukhari, Sahih al-. Sahih al-Bukhari. Trans. Muhammad Muhsin Khan. Accessed June 8, 2025.

Du Ryer, André. L'Alcoran de Mahomet. Paris: A de Sommaville, 1647. https://fr.wikisource.org/wiki/L'Alcoran_(Traduction_de_Du_Ryer)

Guillaume, Alfred, trans. The Life of Muhammad: A Translation of Ibn Ishaq's Sirat Rasul Allah. Oxford: Oxford University Press, 1967.

Hilali, Muhammad Taqi-ud-Din, and Muhammad Muhsin Khan, trans. The Noble Quran: English Translation of the Meanings and Commentary. Medina: King Fahd Complex, 2013.

Ibn Kathir. Al-Bidayahh an Nihayah 'A Mention of Mohammed's Slave Boys and Slave Girls' (pg.1877-89) Trans. Darussalam, 2010.

Ibn Kathir. Stories of the Prophets. Trans. Rashad Ahmad Azami. Riyadh: Darussalam, 2003.

Ibn Kathir. Tafsir Ibn Kathir. Trans. Safiur-Rahman al-Mubarakpuri. 10 vols. Riyadh: Darussalam, 2000.

Ibn Majah. Sunan Ibn Majah. Trans. Nasiruddin al-Khattab.

Keller, Nuh Ha Mim, trans. Reliance of the Traveller: A Classic Manual of Islamic Sacred Law. Beltsville, MD: Amana Publications, 2015.

Muir, William. The Life of Mohammad from Original Sources. Edinburgh: John Grant, 1923.

Muslim, Sahih. Sahih Muslim. Trans. Abdul Hamid Siddiqui.

Pickthall, Muhammad Marmaduke. The Meaning of the Glorious Quran: An Explanatory Translation. New York: Knopf, 1930.

Secondary Sources:

A Common Word Between Us and You. Open letter from 138 Muslim scholars to Christian leaders. 13 October 2007.

AAOIFI. Shari'ah Standards. Accounting and Auditing Organization for Islamic Financial Institutions, 2017. Section 35(9), p. 896.

al Fadi, ed. The Qur'an Dilemma: Former Muslims Analyze Islam's Holiest Book. Vol. 1. 2011.

An Explanatory Memorandum: From the Archives of the Muslim Brotherhood in America. Gov't Exhibit 003-0085, U.S. v. Holy Land Foundation et al., 2013.

Awang, Abdul Hadi. "Perpaduan Ummah Merentasi Idealogi." Speech, Malasia, 26 November 2016. https://tariqlurus.blogspot.com/2016/11/perpaduan-ummah-merentasi-idealogi.html

Aziz, Molvi Abdul. Islamic Studies: Grades 1-12. 12 vols. Darussalam, 2010-2011.

Bagby, Ihsan. The American Mosque 2020: Growing and Evolving. Institute for Social Policy and Understanding, 2021.

BBC News. Halala: The Men Who Sell Divorce. Documentary, 2017.

BBC News. Iraq's Secret Sex Trade: Undercover with the Clerics. Documentary, 2019.

Brubaker, Daniel A. Corrections in Early Qur'an Manuscripts: Twenty Examples. Think and Tell Press, 2019.

Brown, Jonathan A.C. Hadith: Muhammad's Legacy in the Medieval and Modern World. 2nd ed. Oneworld Publications, 2021.

Burton, Richard F. Personal Narrative of a Pilgrimage to Al-Madinah & Meccah. Vol 1. & II. George Bell & Sons, London, 1907.

Carney, Mark. Speech at Eid al-Adha celebration hosted by the Muslim Association of Canada. Ottawa, 6 June 2025. https://www.youtube.com/watch?v=SKLmXKXc0Ms

Chirac, Jacques. Press conference, Algiers, 1 December 2001. Official transcript, Présidence de la République.

Chowdhury, Safaruk Z. A Treatise on Disputation and Argument (Risalat al-Adab fi 'Ilm al-Bahth wa'l-Munazara). Dar al-Nicosia, 2020.

Cottee, Simon. The Apostates: When Muslims Leave Islam. Hurst & Company, 2015.

Coughlin, Stephen. "Bridge-Building" to Nowhere: The Catholic Church's Case Study in Interfaith Delusion. Center for Security Policy, 2015.

Crimp, Richard, and Joel Richardson, eds. Why We Left Islam: Former Muslims Speak Out. WND Books, 2008.

Darwish, Nonie. Cruel and Unusual Punishment. Thomas Nelson, 2008.

Davis, Robert C. Christian Slaves, Muslim Masters. Palgrave Macmillan, 2004.

Dieppe, Tim. The Challenge of Islam: Understanding and Responding to Islam's Increasing Influence in the UK. 2025.

Ellinger, Elaine. A Civilizational Reckoning: Understanding the Threat, Reclaiming the Future. POI Publishing, 2025.

Ellinger, Elaine. Timeless Essays About Islam and Its Doctrine: What It Includes and Why It Matters. POI Publishing, 2024.

Emerick, Yahiya. How to Tell Others about Islam. Amirah Publishing, 2010.

Emerick, Yahiya. What Islam Is All About. Amirah Publishing, 2000.

Fatourechi, Max. Diary of a Revolution. 2025.

Fernández-Morera, Darío. The Myth of the Andalusian Paradise: Muslims, Christians, and Jews under Islamic Rule in Medieval Spain. ISI Books, 2016.

Gabriel, Mark A. Jesus and Muhammad: Profound Differences and Surprising Similarities in the Lives and Teachings of Jesus and Muhammad. Front Line Publishing, 2004.

Gawthrop, William. The Criminal Investigator: Intelligence Analyst's Handbook of Islam. Outskirts Press, 2006.

Goel, Sita Ram. Heroic Hindu Resistance to Muslim Invaders: 636 AD to 1206 AD. Voice of India, 1984.

Hirsi Ali, Ayaan. The Challenge of Dawa: Political Islam as Ideology and Movement and How to Counter It. Hoover Institution Press, 2017.

Holy Bible: New International Version (NIV). Zondervan, 2011.

Hoyland, Robert G. Seeing Islam as Others Saw It. Darwin Press, 1997.

Husain, Ed. Among the Mosques. 2021.

Ibrahim, Raymond. Sword and Scimitar: Fourteen Centuries of War Between Islam and the West. Grand Central Publishing, 2018.

Karch, Efraim. Islamic Imperialism: A History. Yale University Press, 2007.

Kassam, Raheem. No Go Zones. Regnery Publishing, 2017.

Khomeini, Ruhollah. Tahrir al-Wasilah (Exposition of the Means). Trans. Sayyid Ali Reza Naqavi. Tehran, 2001.

Kirby, Stephen M. Islamic Doctrine Versus the U.S. Constitution: The Dilemma for Muslim Public Officials. Center for Security Policy Press, 2020.

Klar, Christian. Was ist los in unseren Schulen?: Ein Schulreport. Seifert Verlag, 2024.

Lane, William A. Manners and Customs of the modern Egyptians. Alexander Garner, 1895.

Locke, John. A Letter Concerning Toleration. Translated by William Popple. London, 1689.

Luxenberg, Christoph. The Syro-Aramaic Reading of the Quran. Verlag Hans Schiler, 2007.

Menezes, J.L. The Life and Religion of Mohammed, the Prophet of Arabia. Originally published 1912.

Merriam-Webster Dictionary. "Creed."

Mission Dawah. Pocket Dawah Manual. Mission Dawah, 2013.
Morris, Benny, and Dror Ze'evi. The Thirty-Year Genocide: Turkey's Destruction of Its Christian Minorities, 1894-1924. Harvard University Press, 2019.
Murray, Douglas. The Strange Death of Europe: Immigration, Identity, Islam. Bloomsbury, 2017.
Nelson Intercepted Letters. Copies of Original Letters from the Army of General Bonaparte in Egypt. London: J. Wright, 1798–1800. Vol. 1.
Nongbri, Brent. Before Religion: A History of a Modern Concept. New Haven: Yale University Press, 2013. (pp. 38-45)
Nushuz. Born a Burden: Breaking Free from Islam, Tradition, and Silence. 2025.
Nystrom. Atlas of Canada and the World. Herff Jones Education Division, 2006.
Poole, Sophia K. The Englishwoman in Egypt: Letters from Cairo. Zieber & Co., 1845.
Pressburg, Norbert G. What the Modern Martyr Should Know: Seventy-Two Grapes and Not a Single Virgin. Norbert Publishers, 2012.
Saleem, Muhammad. Islamic Banking – A $300 Billion Deception. Xlibris, 2006.
Sénatus-consulte du 14 juillet 1865. Napoleon III https://fr.wikisource.org/wiki/S%C3%A9natus-consulte_du_14_juillet_1865_sur_l%27%C3%A9tat_des_personnes_et_la_naturalisation_en_Alg%C3%A9rie
Shaw, Leslie James. Allah au Boulot: L'islam politique sur le lieu de travail. [Islam at Work]2020.
Siddiqi, Shamim A. Methodology of Da'wah Ilallah in American Perspective. The Forum for Islamic Work, 1989.
Solomon, Sal, and Elias Al-Maqdisi. The Mosque Exposed. ANM Press, 2008.
Solomon, Sal, and Elias Al-Maqdisi. Al-Yahud: Eternal Islamic Enmity & the Jews. 24:14 World Publishing, 2023.

Sookhdeo, Patrick. Understanding Shari'a Finance: The Muslim Challenge to Western Economics. Isaac Publishing, 2008.
Spencer, Robert. The History of Jihad: From Muhammad to ISIS. Bombardier Books, 2018.
Spencer, Robert. Muhammad: A Critical Biography. Bombardier Books, 2024.
The Tanakh. English translation.
Toledano, Ehud R. Slavery and Abolition in the Ottoman Middle East. University of Washington Press, 1997.
Trofimov, Yaroslav. The Siege of Mecca. Doubleday, 2008.
Watt, W. Montgomery. Muhammad at Medina. Oxford University Press, 1956.
Webb, Simon. The Forgotten Slave Trade: The White European Slaves of Islam. Pen & Sword Books, 2021.
Wiktionary. "Creedism." August 2024.
Voice of America video Earnie Porta mayor invites adhan https://www.youtube.com/watch?v=vgOShYiBHOQ
Ye'or, Bat. The Decline of Eastern Christianity Under Islam: From Jihad to Dhimmitude. Fairleigh Dickinson University Press, 1996.
Ye'or, Bat. The Dhimmi. Associated University Press, 1985.

Selected Reports

A Common Word Between Us and You. Royal Aal al-Bayt Institute for Islamic Thought, Amman, Jordan, 13 October 2007.
Abdallah et al. The Multiplicity of Halal Standards: A Case Study of Application to Slaughterhouses. Journal of Ethnic Foods, 2021.
An Explanatory Memorandum: From the Archives of the Muslim Brotherhood in America. Gov't Exhibit 003-0085, U.S. v. Holy Land Foundation et al.
ARTICLE 19. U.N. Resolution 16/18: Critical Briefing by ARTICLE 19. 2013.
Banks, Emily, et al. "Female Genital Mutilation and Obstetric Outcome: WHO Collaborative Prospective Study in Six

African Countries." The Lancet 367, no. 9525 (2006): 1835-184.
Burgess, Scott (trans.). The Muslim Brotherhood "Project". Translation of text from Sylvain Besson, La conquête de l'Occident: Le projet secret des Islamistes, Paris: Le Seuil, 2005, pp. 193–205. Investigative Project Archives.
CAIR California – 2023 Annual Report.
Cairo Declaration of Human Rights https://cdn.oic-apps.org/documents/pages/legal/conventions/oic_conventions_cairo_declaration_en.pdf
Charter of the Scholars of the Ummah Concerning the Flood of al-Aqṣā. Issued June 2025. Translated by MEMRI. (Fatwa)
Constitution of the Federal Republic of Nigeria. 1999 (as amended). Sections 275 and 277. https://constituteproject.org/constitution/Nigeria_2011
Constitution of Kenya. 2010. Article 170. https://klrc.go.ke/index.php/constitution-of-kenya/133-chapter-ten-judiciary/136-part-3-subordinate-courts/339-170-kadhis-courts
Davidson, Christopher. A Degree of Influence: The Funding of Strategically Important Subjects in UK Universities. 2021.
EU Parliamentary Assembly. Sharia, the Cairo Declaration and the European Convention on Human Rights. Section #8 on Sharia Courts. https://assembly.coe.int/nw/xml/XRef/Xref-XML2HTML-en.asp?fileid=25353
Flynn, Julian The Global Prevalence of Female Genital https://cspi-web-media.ams3.cdn.digitaloceanspaces.com/documents/CSPI_FGM_INDEX_2025.pdf
FOX 2 Detroit, 9–10 September 2025 coverage of Dearborn City Council meeting.
French Government. Frères musulmans et islamisme politique en France: Le rapport du Gouvernement. Paris: Premier Ministre, Délégation interministérielle à la laïcité, May 2025.
Hansard. Islamophobia Definition. U.K. Parliament, 2021.

Holbrook, Donald. Sacred Violence: The Enduring Role of Ideology in Terrorism and Radicalisation. U.K. Commission for Countering Extremism, 2025.

Institute for the Study of Global Antisemitism and Policy (ISGAP). Cornell: Ten Billion Dollar University (March 2024).

Institute for the Study of Global Antisemitism and Policy (ISGAP). Follow the Money (2020), Volumes I & II.

Islamic Republic of Iran. The Constitution of the Islamic Republic of Iran (1979, amended 1989).

Kirby, Steve. Ongoing Concerns About Muslim American Mosques and Events. March 2025.

MCDC Countering Hybrid Warfare Project: Countering Hybrid Warfare 2019.

MCDC Countering Hybrid Warfare Project: Countering Hybrid Warfare 2017.

MCDC Multi-Domain Multinational Understanding, 2022.

Merley, S. Extremism and the Council on American-Islamic Relations (CAIR) 2007.

NCCM Green Square Campaign Educator's Handbook. 2024

Polis. Acceptance Campaign for Diversity and Self-Determination in Islam Launched, 2026 https://www.ak-polis.de/ich-bin-muslim-akzeptanzkampagne-im-islam/

Sewell, Gilbert T. Islam in the Classroom, What the Textbooks Tell Us. American Textbook Council, 2008.

Shafiq, Muhammad & Mohammed Abu-Nimer (eds.). Interfaith Dialogue: A Guide for Muslims. International Institute for Islamic Thought, 2007.

Solomon, Sal. Islamization Through Halal Products. Christian Concern, 2019.

Swedish Government, Prohibition of Marriage Between Cousins and Certain Other Close Relatives, Ministry of Justice, Ds 2024:17. English translation.

U.K. Commons. Islamophobia Report, 2024.

U.K. House of Commons Library, Sharia Law Courts. 2019.

U.N. Human Rights Council. Resolution 16/18: Combating Religious Intolerance. A/HRC/RES/16/18, 24 March 2011.

United Nations. Universal Declaration of Human Rights. 1948.

U.S. Commission on International Religious Freedom. Shari'ah Criminal Law in Northern Nigeria. 2019.

Wagner, William. Political Islam, Sharia Law, and the American Constitution. Salt & Light Global, 2016.

Wimhurst. 'Nothing to Do With Islam'. Indo-Pacific Strategic Papers, 2016.

World Health Organization. *Female Genital Mutilation.* Fact Sheet. Geneva: World Health Organization. Updated 2025.

World Health Organization. Female Genital Mutilation and Obstetric Outcome.

About the Author

Elaine Ellinger is a Canadian researcher, author, and educator whose work examines Islamic doctrine and its consequences for Western societies, particularly for non-Muslims, but also for Muslims living under or affected by Sharia. Her interest in the subject began in 1983 through conversations with refugees and was shaped by a career in social services, including child protection and support for victims of sexual abuse.

Raised in a home that welcomed dozens of foster brothers and sisters from diverse backgrounds, Elaine developed a lifelong commitment to human dignity and an enduring opposition to coercion, cruelty, and the abuse of power.

She has written more than one hundred articles and produced educational videos and podcasts examining Sharia, jihad, dawa, Islamic governance, and the historical development of Islamic jurisprudence through Islam's own primary sources. She has addressed politicians, academics, students, and public audiences in Canada and internationally, and is the founder of Perspectives on Islam. She previously served as Canadian Director of the Center for the Study of Political Islam International.

Elaine is the author of A Civilizational Reckoning: Understanding the Threat, Reclaiming the Future, an examination of Islamic doctrine, Sharia, historical precedent, legal structures, and the mechanisms through which Islamic law advances within Western societies. The book concludes by proposing legislative and policy measures available to democratic states seeking to preserve freedom of belief while preventing the establishment of parallel legal systems rooted in Sharia.

She is also the author of The Hidden Curriculum of Islamic Schools, which examines Islamic Studies textbooks for Grades 1-12, together with supplementary teaching materials, prepared specifically for Muslim students in English-speaking Western countries attending full-time Islamic schools, weekend programmes, and home-schooling. Comparing these texts with the Quran, hadith, classical tafsir, and authoritative works of Islamic jurisprudence, it documents how Islamic doctrine, Sharia, identity, and attitudes toward non-Muslims are conveyed to children while the legal and political dimensions of Islam are frequently omitted or minimized.

Across her books, articles, lectures, and public presentations, Elaine's research examines the growing influence of Sharia within Western institutions - including education, media, the courts, finance, and government - and the reluctance of political and institutional leaders to examine its doctrinal foundations critically.

Acknowledgements

I want to thank the many people with whom I have spoken and worked over the years on this subject. Your knowledge, questions, and willingness to share your experiences have enriched this work in countless ways.

Particular thanks are due to my reviewers, and to the individuals and platforms prepared to engage difficult subjects and place public education and the pursuit of truth ahead of entertainment, fashionable narratives, or commercial interests. At a time when serious examination of doctrine and its consequences is often avoided, your commitment to providing a forum for evidence-based discussion and critical inquiry demonstrates both integrity and courage.

www.ingramcontent.com/pod-product-compliance
Lightning Source LLC
LaVergne TN
LVHW050817061126
851857LV00012B/848
9781069847256